Bachs Leipziger Kinder
Bach's Children in Leipzig

Die Faksimiles aller Taufzettel sind als hochwertige Drucke exklusiv zu beziehen bei:

Verein Thomaskirche – Bach 2000, Thomaskirchhof 18, 04109 Leipzig
Tel.: 0049 (0) 341 – 22 22 42 50
E-Mail: verein@thomaskirche.org

Wir danken für die freundliche Unterstützung:
dem Bach-Archiv Leipzig
der Universitätsbibliothek Leipzig

Die Deutsche Bibliothek – Bibliographische Information
Die Deutsche Bibliothek verzeichnet diese Publikation in der Deutschen Nationalbibliographie; detaillierte bibliographische Daten sind im Internet über http://dnb.ddb.de abrufbar.

© 2008 by Evangelische Verlagsanstalt GmbH, Leipzig
Printed in Germany · H 7198
Alle Rechte vorbehalten
Cover: Kai-Michael Gustmann, Leipzig
unter Verwendung von Scherenschnitten aus dem Bach-Archiv Leipzig
Layout: behnelux gestaltung, Halle/Saale
Druck und Binden: Druckerei Böhlau, Leipzig

ISBN 978-3-374-02505-3
www.eva-leipzig.de

Martin Petzoldt

Bachs Leipziger Kinder

Dokumente von Johann Sebastian Bachs eigener Hand

Bach's Children in Leipzig

Documents in Johann Sebastian Bach's Own Hand

Translated into English by Hans Hillerbrand, Stefanie Wollny,
Raymond Hinrichs and Andreas Model

EVANGELISCHE VERLAGSANSTALT
Leipzig

Taufstein der Thomaskirche mit dem 1945 verloren gegangenen Deckel

Baptismal font of the St. Thomas Church with its ornate cover, lost in 1945

Das Archiv der Thomaskirche zu Leipzig besitzt einen einzigartigen Schatz. In gleichmäßigen Kästchen aus Karton werden Tausende von Taufzetteln aufbewahrt – einfach oder zweifach gefaltet, etwa von 1699 an beginnend. In dieser Sammlung enthalten sind 15 Zettel, die mit Johann Sebastian Bach in Beziehung stehen, zwölf davon betreffen Bachs Leipziger Kinder aus seiner Ehe mit Anna Magdalena. Die Zettel wurden von dem ehemaligen Superintendenten der Thomaskirche Herbert Stiehl (1909–1992) im Jahr 1978 aufgefunden. Sie werden im Verlauf dieser Einführung in Umschrift abgedruckt, mit Nummerierung 1–12 versehen und jeweils mit Zeilenzahl in Klammer zitiert. In kursiver Schrift werden die von einem Schreiber stammenden Passagen wiedergegeben, in normaler Schrift die von Bachs eigener Hand geschriebenen.

Nachdem die Frage nach den beiden Frauen Bachs in den letzten Jahren gestellt und teilweise beantwortet worden ist, eröffnen diese Dokumente nun einen einzigartigen Weg, die Familie Johann Sebastian Bachs näher kennen zu lernen. Mit den zwölf Taufzetteln aus der Thomaskirche halten wir eine kostbare Dokumentensammlung in den Händen, die viel zu berichten vermag über eine Familie, von der sonst nur die musikalischen Söhne in das Blickfeld der Öffentlichkeit treten.

The archives of the St. Thomas Church in Leipzig hold a unique treasure. Thousands of baptismal "slips", beginning with the year 1699, are stored – folded once or twice – in small cardboard boxes of equal size. Fifteen of these slips relate to Johann Sebastian Bach and are part of this collection. Twelve concern Bach's children, born in Leipzig of his marriage with Anna Magdalena. The baptismal slips were discovered in 1978 by Herbert Stiehl (1909–1992), the former superintendent of St. Thomas. They are reproduced in this introduction, marked as numbers 1 to 12 with the line numbers given in brackets. The parish clerk's notations are printed in italics, the words written by Bach in normal font.

In recent years questions about Bach's wives and children have received considerable attention. The paper slips found in these cardboard boxes offer a unique opportunity to gain insights into Johann Sebastian Bach's family. The twelve baptismal slips from St. Thomas represent a precious collection of documents that throw light on a family otherwise only in the public eye for its musical sons.

Wozu sich ein Zettelkasten auf der Kanzel der Leipziger Thomaskirche befand

Alle diese Taufzettel hatten offensichtlich zwei verschiedene Funktionen: Einmal dienten sie der Abkündigung innerhalb des umfänglichen Fürbitten- und Gebetsteils am Schluss des Kanzeldienstes während aller Frühgottesdienste der Sonntage – nicht der Festtage. Diese Gottesdienste hatte in der Regel der Thomaspastor, Inhaber der ersten Stelle an der Kirche, in der Thomaskirche zu halten. Zum andern aber dienten die Taufzettel zur Vorlage der Eintragung im Taufbuch der Thomaskirche.

Aus dem noch vorhandenen liturgischen Merkbuch, das Johann Christoph Rost (1676–1739) mit seinem Dienstantritt als Thomasküster im Jahr 1716 anlegte, wissen wir von einem „Kästlein", das auf der Kanzelbrüstung angebracht war. In dieses hatte der Küster für jeden Frühgottesdienst der Sonntage alle die Zettel zu legen, die in bestimmter Reihenfolge „abgelesen", d. h. ihrem Inhalt nach bekannt gegeben werden mussten. Im Einzelnen handelte es sich um recht Verschiedenartiges, was da mitzuteilen war, bedenkt man nur, dass in Zeiten noch ohne das früheste Massenmedium regelmäßiger Tageszeitungen gottesdienstliche Abkündigungen – einmal je Woche – die einzige Gelegenheit der öffentlichen Information für einen Ort, eine Stadt bzw. eine Stadtgemeinde war. Neben der Ankündigung von besonde-

The Slip Collection Box in the Pulpit of St. Thomas in Leipzig

These baptismal slips apparently served two different functions. For one, they were used as a reference for announcements for the intercessory prayer at the end of the worship service. Such announcements were only made during the Sunday morning services and not on holidays. As a rule, these services were conducted by the pastor of St. Thomas, who held the highest position in the church. Secondly, the baptismal slips served as sources for entries in the parish register of St. Thomas.

We know of the existence of a small box, attached to the pulpit banister, from the liturgical and worship schedule book begun by Johann Christoph Rost (1676–1739) when he assumed the position of sexton at St. Thomas in 1716. In preparation for the Sunday morning service, it was the sexton's responsibility to place the relevant slips into the small box. These slips had to be "read", i. e. announced, in a certain order. The information conveyed varied greatly, as one must bear in mind that in those days, previous even to of such early mass media as regular daily newspapers, weekly announcements in the Sunday morning service were often the only means by which news could be passed on to a wider public in village, town, or borough. Besides the announcement of special holidays, commemo-

ren Fest- oder Gedenktagen des Jahres, von Geburtstagen, Hochzeiten, Trauerfällen und Reisen der kurfürstlichen Familie, der Verlesung von politischen Mandaten und Ordnungen, wie etwa zweimal im Jahr die Eheordnung, von Warnungen vor Dieben und marodierenden Banden, kirchlichen Mitteilungen, hatten insbesondere auch Personalnachrichten der Kommune ihren Platz, die durch bestellte Fürbitten und Gebetsanliegen oder durch vollzogene Taufen (was gleichbedeutend war für die Mitteilung der Geburt), Trauungen und Beerdigungen bedingt waren. Und hier hatten diese Taufzettel Platz und Funktion.

Was auf einem Taufzettel vermerkt wurde

Schaut man sich die Taufzettel an, so enthalten sie bei großer Verschiedenheit des Aufgeschriebenen nach Reihenfolge und Formulierungen folgende Informationen: Tag der Taufe des Kindes, Verzeichnung der Eltern und der Paten jeweils mit vollständigen Titeln, Namen und Berufsangaben, bei Frauen, die rechtlich von Männern der Familie – Väter, Ehemänner, Brüder oder Söhne – abhängig waren, ihre Herkunft, ihr sozialer Stand und ihr Geburtsname. Waren Paten nicht anwesend, wurde sie durch stellvertretende Paten ersetzt; und auch diese wurden sorgsam vermerkt, wie die Taufzettel 2 (30–31) und 5 (94–98) zeigen. Dann ist der Name des Täuflings

rations, birthdays, weddings, deaths, travels of the prince-elector's family, as well as political mandates and legal regulations – for example twice yearly the marriage regulations had to be read, as well as public warnings of thieves and marauding gangs, not to mention ecclesiastic announcements – the personal news of the community had their particular space here. The announcements included requests for intercessions and prayers, baptisms (which were equivalent to birth announcements), weddings and funerals. In this context the baptismal slips had their specific place and function.

The Information Found on the Baptismal Slips

A closer look at the baptismal slips suggests that they varied greatly with respect to the order and wording of the information. The slips recorded the day of the child's baptism, the parents and godparents with complete titles, names and professions, and in the case of women (who were legally subject to the men of the family, e.g. fathers, husbands, brothers or sons) their origin, social status, and maiden name. If godparents were not actually present at the baptism, they were represented by delegated godparents; and these, too, were carefully identified, as can be seen on the baptismal slips nos. 2 (30–31) and 5 (94–98). Next, the name of the child to be

aufgeschrieben, oft ausdrücklich mit der Formel eingeführt: „Des Kindes Name soll sein" bzw. „Das Kind soll heißen". Im Anschluss an diese Daten folgte schließlich eine Registrierangabe, in der eine doppelte Nummer festgehalten wurde: über einem Strich die Zahl der Taufe des betreffenden Monats, unter dem Strich die Zahl der Taufe im laufenden Jahr. Dann folgt das damals noch allgemein übliche Zeichen für den jeweiligen Wochentag, an dem die Taufe stattfand:

- ☉ Sonntag
- ☽ Montag
- ♂ Dienstag
- ☿ Mittwoch
- ♃ Donnerstag
- ♀ Freitag
- ♄ Sonnabend

Nun vermerkte der Schreiber – meist in Kürzeln – den Namen des Täufers, versehen mit seinem erworbenen akademischen Titel, nicht aber mit dem kirchlichen, also Doctor (D.), Licentiatus (L. oder Lic.), Magister (M.). Was von diesen Einzelheiten im Falle der sonntäglichen Abkündigung und Einbeziehung in Fürbitten alles verlesen wurde und was allein für den Schreiber des Kirchenbuchs bestimmt war, also auf der Kanzel weggelassen wurde, ist nicht mehr völlig aufzuklären. Sicher aber wurde auf Namen und Stand der Eltern, Namen des Kindes und Datum der Taufe nicht verzichtet, denn sie gehörten in den Zusammenhang der Fürbitt- und Dankgebete.

baptized is recorded, often specifically introduced with the phrase "The child's name shall be ..." or alternatively "The child shall be called ..." This is followed by a specific registration mark consisting of two members separated by a line: above it the number of baptisms of that particular month, and below the line the number of baptisms in the current year. This was followed by a symbol commonly used at that time to indicate the week day on which the baptism took place:

- ☉ Sunday;
- ☽ Monday;
- ♂ Tuesday;
- ☿ Wednesday;
- ♃ Thursday;
- ♀ Friday;
- ♄ Saturday.

Next, the writer noted – mostly in abbreviated terms – the name of the officiating pastor with his acquired academic but not his ecclesiastical titles, i. e. Doctor (D.), Licentiate (L. or Lic.), and Master (M.). It is no longer clear which of these details were actually read during the Sunday announcements and intercessions and which were intended only for the keeper of the parish register and therefore were omitted in the pulpit announcements. But it is certain that the names and family status of the parents, the name of the child and the date of baptism were always read out aloud, because they were relevant for the intercessions and prayers of thanksgiving. All the other

Alle anderen Angaben haben grundsätzliche Bedeutung für die Taufzeugenschaft sowie für das Kirchenbuchwesen, was bis heute wichtig ist z. B. für die Ahnenforschung.

Wer die Taufzettel geschrieben hat
Es begegnen sehr unterschiedliche Handschriften: solche, die als typische Kanzleischriften ausgemacht werden können, aber auch solche, die eine zwar ausgeschriebene, aber nicht sehr ansehnliche Schrift haben. Auf fast allen Zetteln – Ausnahme Taufzettel 12 – hat Bach selbst den Namen des Kindes eingetragen. Die Zettel 5 und 11 sind sogar bis auf wenige Details vollständig von der Hand Bachs geschrieben. Wir haben es also mit einem Bestand an Autographen Bachs zu tun, was nicht nur den Wert der Sammlung wesentlich bestimmt, sondern auch zum Nachdenken anregt über die Praxis der Entstehung eines solchen Taufzettels.

Vermutlich machte sich nach der Geburt eines Kindes ein Familienmitglied – wohl der Vater – auf den Weg, um die Geburt öffentlich bekannt zu geben und damit die Taufe anzumelden, die nach dem Brauch der Zeit meist gleich am Folgetag vollzogen wurde. Man taufte deshalb sehr rasch nach der Geburt, weil die hohe Kindersterblichkeit das Risiko in sich barg, ein Kind könne ungetauft versterben. Deshalb auch besteht seit den Anfängen des Christentums die Berechtigung

details are of particular significance for understanding godparenthood as well as for church records, which continue to be important to this day, e. g. for genealogical research.

Who Wrote the Baptismal Slips?
The slips display different handwritings. Some display typical chancery script, while others are written legibly but appear untidy. On almost all the slips – with the exception of slip no. 12 – Bach wrote the name of the new-born infant himself. Slips nos. 5 and 11 were written entirely by Bach, except for a few details. We therefore have a collection of Bach autographs here, which not only determines the value of the collection but also raises the question of how such baptismal slips came to be written.

Presumably a member of the family – generally the father – went to the ecclesiastical authorities to announce the birth officially and at the same time to register the infant for baptism, which was usually performed on the following day. New-born infants were baptized soon after their birth, as the high infant mortality in those days entailed the risk that they might die without having received the sacrament. For this reason, since the beginnings of Christianity every Christian was entitled and obliged to baptize a weakly or dying child in an emergency. Bach probably exercised this responsibility at the emergency baptism of Regina

9

und Verpflichtung jedes Christen zur Nottaufe eines schwachen oder sterbenden Kindes. Dieses Recht hat bei der Nottaufe des sechsten Kindes zweiter Ehe, Regina Johanna, eventuell Bach selbst ausgeübt (Taufzettel 5). Denn der Vermerk eines Pfarrers, hier des Magisters Justus Gotthard Rabener (1688–1731), kann aber auch allein wegen der Bestätigung der Taufe hinzu gesetzt worden sein, die durch einen Geistlichen zu erfolgen hatte. Das Mädchen überstand zwar die Schwachheit bei der Geburt und wuchs heran, starb aber bereits nach 4 ½ Jahren.

Bei Betrachtung der meisten Taufzettel lag die Vermutung nahe, die Schreiber könnten die Küster der betreffenden Kirche gewesen sein. Da jedoch die bekannten Schriftzüge der beiden zur Zeit Bachs tätigen Thomasküster Johann Christoph Rost, 1716 bis 1739 im Amt, und Christian Köpping, 1741 bis 1772 Küster, nicht vorkommen, richtete sich das Interesse nun auf die Küster-Famuli, was eher unwahrscheinlich sein mochte; doch auch diese Vermutung scheint angesichts der erwachsen und ausgeschrieben wirkenden Schriftzüge nicht zuzutreffen. Jedoch konnte bisher einer der Taufzettel seiner Schrift nach identifiziert werden; es handelt sich um den letzten dieser Reihe, den Taufzettel 12. Dieser wurde nachweislich[1] von dem damaligen Unterleichenschreiber Andreas Gottlieb Bienengräber (1707–1779) geschrieben, einem Angestellten der Stadt. Das

Johanna, the sixth child of his second marriage (see baptismal slip no. 5). The note of a parish pastor, in this case the church magistrate Justus Gotthard Rabener (1688–1731), may have been added to confirm the baptism which otherwise had to be performed by a clergy. Although the infant girl survived her weakness at birth and appeared to be doing well, she died at the age of 4 ½ years.

A look at the baptismal slips suggests that they were usually written by the sextons of the church. However, the known handwriting of either of the two sextons at St. Thomas during Bach's time – Johann Christoph Rost, 1716 to 1739, and Christian Köpping, 1741 to 1772 – does not appear on the baptismal slips. Our attention, therefore, turned to the assistants to the sextons, even though this seemed rather improbable, particularly in view of the elaborate adult handwriting. Still, the writer of one of the baptismal slips could be identified: No. 12 is in the hand of Andreas Gottlieb Bienengräber (1707–1779), a town employee at that time, whose function it was to record deaths.[1] This allows us to conclude that the baptismal slips were written in the judge's chamber at the Leipzig town hall, where the official registers for baptism, marriage, and funerals were kept. Two individuals worked there during Bach's period of service in Leipzig – Johann Georg Lorentz (1685–1740), *Nuntius Juris* and

lässt immerhin den Schluss zu, dass die Taufzettel in der Richterstube auf dem Rathaus zu Leipzig geschrieben wurden, wo zu dieser Zeit auch die Tauf-, Trau- und Leichenbücher geführt wurden. Hier wirkten während der Leipziger Dienstzeit Bachs Johann Georg Lorentz (1685–1740), seines Zeichens Nuntius juris und Oberleichenschreiber, sowie der genannte Andreas Gottlieb Bienengräber, zunächst Unterleichenschreiber, nach 1740 Oberleichenschreiber. So liegt die Annahme nahe, dass die Mehrzahl der Taufzettel – also außer den Zetteln 2, 5, 11 und 12 – von Johann Georg Lorentz geschrieben worden ist.

Was wir von der Familie Bach in ihrer Leipziger Zeit wissen

Als Bach die Stelle des Thomaskantors und Director musices am 30. Mai 1723 antrat, stand er im 39. Lebensjahr, war nach dem Tod seiner ersten Frau Maria Barbara (1684–1720) Anfang Juli 1720 nunmehr seit 18 Monaten erneut verheiratet mit Anna Magdalena, geborene Wilcke (1701–1760). Die Eheleute waren in Köthen am 3. Dezember 1721 getraut worden. Anna Magdalena war 1701 geboren, also 16 Jahre jünger als Bach, und trat sogleich als Stiefmutter von vier heranwachsenden Kindern aus Bachs erster Ehe in das strenge Reglement familiärer Pflichten ein: Dorothea Catharina (14), Wilhelm Friedemann (12), Carl Philipp Emanuel (9) und Johann Gottfried Bernhard (8) wurden zu ihren

principal copyist of funeral records as well as the above-mentioned Andreas Gottlieb Bienengräber, who started out as Lorentz' assistant and in 1740 succeeded him in his office. It appears reasonable, therefore, to assume that the majority of the baptismal slips – except for nos. 2, 5, 11 and 12 – were written by Johann Georg Lorentz.

Bach's Family During His Time in Leipzig

When Bach took up the position of cantor and *director musices* of St. Thomas on May 30, 1723, he was in the 39th year of his life. After the death of his first wife Maria Barbara (1684–1720) in July 1720, he had married Anna Magdalena Wilcke (1701–1760) in Köthen on December 3, 1721. Born in 1701, Anna was 16 years younger than Bach. She immediately entered the strict regiment of family responsibilities, becoming the stepmother of the four adolescent children from Bach's first marriage: Dorothea Catharina (14), Wilhelm Friedemann (12), Carl Philipp Emanuel (9) and Johann Gottfried Bernhard (8). Maria Barbara's oldest sister,

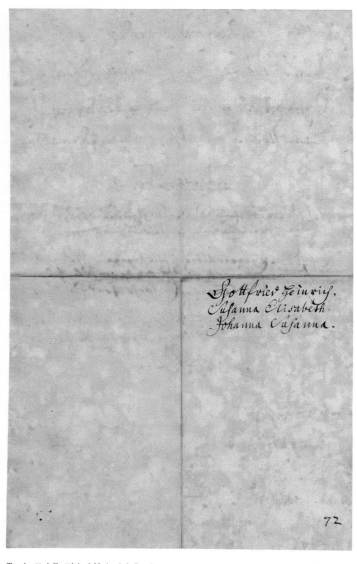

Taufzettel Gottfried Heinrich Bach

Baptismal slip of Gottfried Heinrich Bach

Zu S: Thomas d. 7. Febr: 1724

Vater: H: Johann Sebastian Bach, Director Musices u. Cantor z. Sch: Thom:

Dessen Eheliche Frau Anna Magdalena gebohrne Wülckin

Kindes Nahme Gottfried Heinrich

Pathen.

1./ H: Hofrath D: Gottfried Lange, Bürger-Meister alhier.

2./ Frau Regina Maria geb. M. Johann Heinrich Ernesti, P.P. und des Schul. zu St: Thomæ Rectoris Frau Eheliebste.

3./ H: D: Friedrich Heinrich Graff, des Ober-Hoffgerichts alhier Advocatus Ordinarius.

NB 32/72   C. H. L. S.

Stiefkindern. Im Haushalt befanden sich seit Weimarer Jahren ebenso die älteste unverheiratet gebliebene Schwester Maria Barbaras, Friedelena Margaretha Bach (1675–1729), inzwischen im 49. Lebensjahr, wie auch ein bis zwei Mägde, deren Namen wir nicht kennen. Anna Magdalena hatte noch vor ihrer Ankunft in Leipzig ihr erstes Kind zur Welt gebracht, das zu diesem Zeitpunkt am Leben war, aber bis heute nicht durch einen Taufeintrag nachzuweisen, sondern nur aufgrund des Leipziger Begräbniseintrages von 1726 bekannt ist. Diesem Kind folgten in Leipzig 12 weitere, von denen nur sechs das Erwachsenenalter erreichten. Die Kommentierung der Taufzettel wird uns mit ihrem Schicksal näher vertraut machen.

Als Thomaskantor bewohnte Bach mit seiner Familie – ebenso wie der Thomasschulrektor – eine Dienstwohnung im Gebäude am Thomaskirchhof, das mit seinen großen Räumen nicht nur als Schule, sondern in seinen Dachregionen auch als Alumnat für diejenigen Thomasschüler diente, die im später Thomanerchor genannten Schülerchor mitsangen. Die Kantorenwohnung dehnte sich an der Südseite des Gebäudes über drei Etagen aus, und es dürfte das als „Komponierstube" ausgewiesene Zimmer in der äußersten südwestlichen Ecke der ersten Etage wohl eines der wenigen ruhigeren Zimmer des Hauses gewesen sein. Zwischen-

Friedelena Margaretha Bach (1675–1729) in all likelihood joined the household in Weimar in 1709. She was 49 years of age and remained single for her entire life. There also were one or two maids, whose names are unknown. Prior to her arrival in Leipzig, Anna Magdalena gave birth to her first child, of whom no baptismal record exists, only the record of a funeral in 1726. Anna Magdalena's first child was followed by twelve others, of whom only six reached adulthood. The notes on the baptismal slips allow us to become more familiar with their lives.
As cantor of St. Thomas, Bach lived with his family – just like the rector – in an official apartment in the school building next to St. Thomas. With its large rooms the building not only served as day school, but in the attic also provided accommodation for those pupils boarding at St. Thomas who sang in the school choir, which later was called Thomanerchor. The cantor's flat extended over three floors on the southern side of the building. The room labeled the "composing chamber" was situated in the southwestern corner of the second floor and may have been one of the few quiet rooms in the entire building. From mid-April of 1731 to early June of 1732 the living quarters, the boarding school, and the class and meeting rooms had to be vacated for over a year, because the building, almost 180 years old, was renovated and expanded. For the

zeitlich mussten von Mitte April 1731 bis Anfang Juni 1732 die Wohnungen der Thomasschule, das Alumnat und die Unterrichts- und Versammlungsräume für ein reichliches Jahr geräumt werden, weil das fast 180 Jahre alte Gebäude einer Sanierung und Erweiterung unterzogen werden musste. Zur Einweihung der renovierten Schule am 5. Juni 1732 musizierte Bach die Kantate „Froher Tag, verlangte Stunden" (BWV Anh. 18). Leider wurde diese Thomasschule 170 Jahre später trotz des heftigen Protestes der damals noch jungen „Neuen Bachgesellschaft" (gegründet 1900) auf Veranlassung des Stadtrates 1902 abgerissen, sodass damit ein wesentlicher Ort des alltäglichen Wirkens Bachs in Leipzig heute nur noch mit Hilfe von Bildern und Grundrissen vergegenwärtigt werden kann.

Bach geriet mit seiner Familie recht bald in freundschaftliche Verbundenheit zu Persönlichkeiten des öffentlichen Lebens – Kirche, Schule, Stadtrat und Rittergutsbesitzer – in und um Leipzig und zu Nachbarn. Dafür geben u. a. die Wahl des ersten Beichtvaters der Familie, des Thomaspastors Christian Weise d. Ä. (1671–1736), und vor allem die Patenschaften beredte Auskunft, die für die in Leipzig geborenen 12 Kinder bekannt sind. Auf das wachsende und zugleich tragfähige Netz sozial-freundschaftlicher Verknüpfungen im engeren Umkreis der Stadt und des umgebenden Landes

opening ceremony of the renovated school on June 5, 1732 Bach composed the cantata "Froher Tag, verlangte Stunden" (BWV Anh. 18). Unfortunately the building of the St. Thomas School was demolished 170 years later following a decision of the Leipzig town council in 1902, despite the intense protest of the newly formed "Neue Bachgesellschaft" (established in 1900). As a consequence, an essential site of Bach's life in Leipzig today can only be recalled with the help of pictures and ground plans.

Bach and his family soon made friends with their neighbors and with representatives of the church, school, town council and gentry in Leipzig as well as the surrounding areas. This is attested not only by the family's choice of its first confessor, the pastor of St. Thomas, Christian Weise the older (1671–1736), but also by the godparents for the 12 children born in Leipzig. There are also other hints to the growing network of social contacts in the town and the surrounding countryside: the requests for organ examinations in the vicinity of Leipzig (Störmthal 1723, possibly Pomßen 1726/27, Stöntzsch near Pegau 1731/32, Zschortau 1746), Bach's involvement in the edition of the 1736 hymnbook of Zeitz castle, published by the cantor Georg Christian Schemelli (1676–1762), as well as a number of commissions to compose pieces for special occasions. For

gibt es auch noch andere Hinweise: die Aufforderungen zu Orgelprüfungen in der näheren Umgebung Leipzigs (Störmthal 1723, eventuell Pomßen 1726/27, Stöntzsch bei Pegau 1731/32, Zschortau 1746), die Mitarbeit am Zeitzer Schlossgesangbuch 1736, herausgegeben durch den Schlosskantor Georg Christian Schemelli (um 1676–1762) sowie auch besondere Musikaufträge. So ist die im Nachbarhaus wohnende Familie Bose – neben Patenschaften (Taufzettel 7, 10, 11 und 12), musikalischen Interessen und dem Auftrag zu einer Hochzeitskantate – erst vor wenigen Jahren wieder neu in den Blickpunkt des Interesses getreten (vgl. Taufzettel 7).

Neben anderen jüngeren Verwandten des Thomaskantors und seiner Frau, die als Schüler die Thomasschule besuchten – 1724 Johann Heinrich Bach, ein Neffe Johann Sebastians aus Ohrdruf; 1729 Christian Friedrich Meißner, ein Neffe Anna Magdalenas aus Weißenfels; 1737 Johann Ernst Bach, Sohn eines Großvetters Bachs aus Eisenach –, lebte von Oktober 1737 bis Oktober 1742 Bachs Schweinfurter Vetter Johann Elias Bach (1705–1755) im Hause am Thomaskirchhof und leistete Dienste als Hauslehrer für die Kinder und als Privatsekretär des Thomaskantors. Das lenkt den Blick noch auf andere dienstbare Personen aus dem Schülerkreis Bachs, die das Haus zeitweilig zur Heimat hatten. Ein besonderer Termin muss die Hochzeit der Viertgeborenen, Elisabeth

example the Bose family, who lived next door to the Bachs and are known for their multiple godparenthoods (see baptismal slips nos. 7, 10, 11 and 12), their interest in music, and their having commissioned a wedding cantata from Bach, in recent year attracted scholarly interest once again (see baptismal slip no. 7).

Young relatives of the cantor of St. Thomas and his wife, who attended the St. Thomas School as pupils, lived with the Bach family in the house at Thomaskirchhof: In 1724 Johann Heinrich Bach, J. S. Bach's nephew from Ohrdruf; in 1729 Christian Friedrich Meißner, Anna Magdalena's nephew from Weißenfels; in 1737 Johann Ernst Bach, the son of a distant cousin of Bach's from Eisenach, and from October 1737 until October 1742 Johann Elias Bach (1705–1755), Bach's cousin from Schweinfurt, who earned his living as tutor to the children and private secretary to the Thomaskantor. There were also other pupils of Bach who stayed in the house for some time, providing services to the household. A special occasion was the wedding of Bach's fourth child, Elisabeth Juliana Friederica, who on Monday, January 20, 1749, was married at St. Thomas to Johann Christoph Altnickol, a former pupil of Bach, who became organist of St. Wenceslas in Naumburg. When Bach died in 1750, his children Gottfried Heinrich, Johann Christian, Johanna Carolina,

Juliana Friederica, gewesen sein, die am Montag, den 20. Januar 1749, in Leipzig den ehemaligen Schüler Bachs und damaligen Organisten von St. Wenzel in Naumburg, Johann Christoph Altnickol, in der Thomaskirche heiratete. Als Bach 1750 starb, befanden sich zusammen mit der Witwe Anna Magdalena die Kinder Gottfried Heinrich, Johann Christian, Johanna Carolina, Regina Susanna und die älteste Stiefschwester Catharina Dorothea im Hause. Von Wilhelm Friedemann wissen wir, dass er aus dem nahen Halle herzueilte und mit Unterbrechungen bis zum Weihnachtsabend 1750 blieb, was ihm – da die Reise weder beantragt noch genehmigt war – eine disziplinarische Vorladung vor das Kirchenkollegium der Marktkirche von Halle[2] einbrachte.

Regina Susanna, and their oldest stepsister Catharina Dorothea were still living at home. Wilhelm Friedemann hurried to Leipzig from nearby Halle and, with a few interruptions, stayed with his family until Christmas Eve 1750, which resulted in a disciplinary summons before the ecclesiastical consistory of the Market Church in Halle since his journey and absence had been neither applied for nor approved.[2]

Wie Bachs Kinder aus der ersten Ehe in der Familie lebten
Wenn von Bachs Kindern gesprochen wird, so treten gewöhnlich die durch ihre Kunst berühmt gewordenen Musikersöhne in den Blick. Zu ihnen gehören unbedingt zwei Söhne erster Ehe, Wilhelm Friedemann und Carl Philipp Emanuel, deren Altersabstand vier Jahre betrug. Hinzuzurechnen ist Johann Gottfried Bernhard, von dem leider keine Kompositionen bekannt sind, der aber weitgehend zusammen mit den beiden anderen aufwuchs. Doch sollte nicht vergessen werden, dass der jungen Familie in Weimar an einem der letzten Tage des Jahres 1708

The Children of Bach's First Marriage
When talking about Bach's children, one tends to think primarily of those of his sons who became famous musicians in their own right. The two sons from Bach's first marriage, Wilhelm Friedemann and Carl Philipp Emanuel, born four years apart, are the first who come to mind. Unfortunately, no compositions of Johann Gottfried Bernhard are known, even though he grew up with his two other brothers. It should not be forgotten, however, that on one of the last days in 1708 a girl was born, the first child of the young family; **Catharina Dorothea** (1708–1774), remained in the Bach

als erstes Kind ein Mädchen, **Catharina Dorothea** (1708–1774), geboren wurde, die fast lebenslang als familiäre Hilfe zu Hause blieb. Diese älteste Tochter spielt in der Geschichte der Musikerfamilie Bach mangels einschlägiger Daten nirgends die Rolle, die ihr zukäme, und das, obwohl doch Bach 1730 an den Jugendfreund Georg Erdmann von ihr in allzu großer Bescheidenheit und in untertreibender Formulierung geschrieben hatte, dass musikalisch „auch meine älteste Tochter nicht schlimm [d. h. ganz gut] einschläget"[3]. Das geschieht in einem Zusammenhang, in dem Bach Musikalität und praktische Musikausübung seiner Familie vorstellt und gerade den „sauberen Soprano" seiner jetzigen Frau Anna Magdalena gelobt hatte. Catharina Dorothea war nur sechs Jahre jünger als ihre Stiefmutter und ist wohl zunehmend – insbesondere 1729 nach dem Tod der zur Familie gehörenden Tante Friedelena Margaretha – in die Verantwortung des größer gewordenen Haushalts einbezogen worden.
Von den drei Söhnen erster Ehe teilt **Wilhelm Friedemann** (1710–1784) als ältester Sohn Bachs das Schicksal erstgeborener Söhne: Auf solche richtet sich, vor allem in älteren Zeiten, ein übergroßes Hoffnungspotential des Vaters oder gar der gesamten Familie. Nicht selten hat das auch zu psychischen Belastungen geführt, die bei sorgsamer Betrachtung bei dem ältesten Bachsohn unzweifelhaft

household nearly all her life, always counted upon to help out with all kinds of chores. In the absence of pertinent sources, this oldest daughter does not play the role she might have in the musical history of the Bach family, even though in 1730 Bach wrote to his childhood friend Georg Erdmann with excessive modesty and understatement that "musically even my oldest daughter is not bad at all," in other words, is very good.[3] Bach made this statement in the context of characterizing the musical disposition and practical musical competence of the members of his family, praising in particular the "clean soprano" of his wife Anna Magdalena. Catharina Dorothea was only six years younger than her stepmother and probably had to assume more and more domestic responsibilities in the ever-growing household, especially after the death of her aunt Friedelena Margaretha in 1729.
Wilhelm Friedemann (1710–1784), one of the three sons of Bach's first marriage, shared the typical fate of oldest sons, particularly in those days, of being the object of exaggerated hopes of his father and his family. Frequently this entailed emotional problems, which can easily be discerned in Bach's oldest son. His enormous intellectual gifts allowed him to assert himself in the eyes not only of his father but increasingly also of a wider audience. On the other hand, it would

wahrnehmbar sind. Doch kam ihm seine hohe Begabung zu Hilfe, mit der er nicht nur vor den Augen seines Vaters, sondern auch zunehmend vor den Augen einer breiteren Öffentlichkeit zu bestehen vermochte. Auf der anderen Seite sieht es aber auch so aus, als ob er den Schatten seines Vaters nie ganz losgeworden sei. In den Jahrzehnten seiner Jugend und seines jungen Erwachsenenalters ließ er sich offenbar auch ganz gern von seinem Vater protegieren, wofür die Bewerbungen nach Dresden und nach Halle interessante Zeugnisse ablegen. So sind die Bewerbungsschreiben für die Stelle an der Dresdner Sophienkirche im Juni 1733 von seinem Vater geschrieben und von Wilhelm Friedemann unterschrieben.[4] In Halle hatte er sich 1746 nur bewerben müssen und wurde unter Verzicht auf das Probespiel wegen der Bekanntheit und Verehrung, die sein Vater dort genoss, angenommen.

Durch sorgsame Aufmerksamkeit beim Abriss der alten Thomasschule zu Leipzig im Jahr 1902 konnte der Leipziger Musikwissenschaftler Bernhard Friedrich Richter (1850–1931) zufällig vier Schulhefte sicherstellen, die man in einer schalldämpfenden Tapetenfütterung vorfand[5]. Die Hefte lassen sich durch entsprechende Einträge datieren; sie stammen aus der Leipziger Zeit und beginnen am 15. November 1723 (Heft 1), am 16. Mai 1725 (Heft 2), am 3. März 1726 (Heft 3) und am 30. April 1727 (Heft 4), enthalten

appear that he never quite succeeded in stepping out of his father's shadow. In his youth and early adulthood he obviously was quite willing to let his father facilitate his career; the applications for positions in Halle and Dresden offer interesting confirmation of this. The letters of application for a position at the Dresden Sophienkirche in June 1733 were written by his father and merely signed by Wilhelm Friedemann.[4] At Halle in 1746 he only had to submit a letter of application and was promptly hired without audition because of the fame and admiration which his father enjoyed in his town.

When the old Thomasschule building was demolished in 1902, the musicologist Bernhard Friedrich Richter (1850–1931) by chance was able to rescue four notebooks which were accidentally discovered in the soundproofing insulation behind the wallpaper.[5] These notebooks contain dated entries – they were begun in Leipzig on November 15, 1723 (notebook 1), May 16, 1725 (notebook 2), March 3, 1726 (notebook 3), and April 30, 1727 (notebook 4). Written by Wilhelm Friedemann, they show the efforts of a nearly 13-year-old, a 14-year-old, a 15-year-old, and a 16-year-old. The last notebook contains an assignment to compose a poem from two Latin distichs, a meter mainly used for epigrams and elegies. It has the following wording:

Thomaskirche und Thomasschule 1732

St. Thomas Church and St. Thomas School 1732

also – soweit sie von Wilhelm Friedemanns Hand sind – Arbeiten des knapp dreizehnjährigen, des vierzehnjährigen, des fünfzehnjährigen und des sechzehnjährigen Wilhelm Friedemann Bach. Im spätesten Heft findet sich die Lösung einer Aufgabe, aus zwei Distichen – jenem Versmaß, das vor allem für Epigramme und Elegien Verwendung fand – ein Gedicht zu formen. Es hat folgenden Wortlaut:

Versus
Mortis metus dispellendus
Quae memori versatur pectore mortis imago
Excruciat corda tristia metu trepido
Sed confirmat mentem studium honestae vitae
Atque secuturi spes sine fine poli.

Nach einer poetisch geformten Übertragung[6] hört sich der Inhalt wie folgt an:

Versus
Die Todesfurcht zu zerstreuen
Das Bild des Todes, das im gedenkenden Herzen lebt,
Mag betrübte Seelen in ängstlicher Furcht quälen,
Aber es stärkt das Streben nach ehrbarem Leben
Und die Hoffnung auf den künftigen ewigen Himmel.

In a poetic translation this would read as follow:[6]

> Verse
> Dispelling the fear of death
> The image of death which lives in the remembering heart,
> May torture sorrowful souls in anxious fear,
> But strengthens the striving for an honorable life
> And the hope for a future eternal heaven.

Unmittelbar beeindruckend ist die Ernsthaftigkeit dieser Zeilen. Sie geben eine Mischung von antik philosophischer Moral und christlicher Ethik wieder. Vor allem fällt die Bereitschaft auf, den Tod einbezogen zu sehen in das Leben, in die Alltäglichkeit des Lebens. Solche Alltäglichkeit kennt den Tod wie einen Erinnerungswert, sicher deshalb, weil er einem wohl schon zu oft begegnet ist. Doch Sterben und Tod eignete immer schon der Eindruck, der Furcht und Angst auslöst, was auch durch Glauben nur schwer zu besiegen ist, doch am ehesten begriffen werden kann. Wir sollten die Ernsthaftigkeit und Reife der Beschäftigung eines Sechzehnjährigen mit dem Gedanken des Todes nicht überbewerten – es könnte ja lediglich eine durch den Unterricht veranlasste Beschäftigung sein. Doch verbietet sich auch jede Unterbewertung, gehörte Wilhelm Friedemann doch neben seiner um zwei Jahre älteren Schwester zu den Kindern der Familie, die den Tod der

The seriousness of these lines is most impressive. They represent a mixture of an ancient philosophical ethos and Christian ethics. Above all, they reflect the willingness to see death as an integrant part of life, of everyday matters of living. This familiarity with death results from all too frequent exposures to it. However, dying and death always cause fear and anxiety, and this can hardly be defeated by faith, but at least through faith it may be understood more readily. We should not overestimate the seriousness and maturity of a sixteen-year-old boy's preoccupation with death, however – after all, this might have been simply a school assignment. On the other hand it should not be underestimated either, because Wilhelm Friedemann and his sister, who was born two years earlier, belonged to those children in the family who had to witness and accept the death of their own mother. The fact that his father started a *Clavier Büch-*

eigenen Mutter bewusst aufnehmen und verarbeiten mussten. Dass sein Vater gerade am Anfang jenes Jahres, in dem die Mutter sterben würde, ein eigenes *Clavier-Büchlein vor Wilhelm Friedemann Bach* anlegte, zeigt auch, dass Johann Sebastian damit begonnen hatte, sich seinem ältesten Sohn stärker zuzuwenden und dessen musikalische Ausbildung in die Hand zu nehmen.

Dazu passt, was nun weiterhin zu beobachten ist, wie man sich im Familienkreis um Leben und Tod der jüngeren Geschwister offenbar Gedanken wie auch Sorgen machte. Darauf verweisen Tatsache und Art jener Zusammenstellung der Namen von Familienangehörigen und Geschwistern, die sich im zweiten Schulheft Wilhelm Friedemanns befindet. Die Eintragungen dehnen sich von der Mitte des Jahres 1725 bis 1726 aus; der fünfzehnjährige Wilhelm Friedemann hatte seinen Namen [1] und den seines Bruders Carl Philipp Emanuel [2] eingetragen, eine fremde kindliche Schrift, von der C. Freyse meint, sie sei von Johann Gottfried Bernhard[7], setzt danach die Namenseintragungen [3–8] wie folgt fort:

[1]   Willhelm: Friedeman Bach.
[2]   Carl. Phillipp. Emanuel. Bach.
[3]   Johann. Gottfried. Bernhard: Bach
[4]   Christina: Sophia: Henrietta: Bachin
        mortua est, die 29 junio: aeta[tis]
                                    3 ¼. 1726
[5]   ~~Joh.~~ Gottfried. Heinrich Bach
[6]   Christin²a¹. Gottlieb Bach
[7]   Johann: Sebastian. Bach
[8]   Friedelena Marg[aretha Bach]

lein vor Wilhelm Friedemann Bach earlier in the year his mother died, suggests that Johann Sebastian Bach had begun to pay greater attention to his oldest son and was preparing to take over his musical education.

In accordance with this, we can observe the concerns and worries in the family about the life and death of the younger siblings. Evidence for this is found in the way Wilhelm Friedemann's second notebook listed and noted the names of family members, brothers and sisters. The entries extend from mid-1725 to 1726; first the fifteen-year-old Wilhelm Friedemann had entered his own name [1] and that of his brother Carl Philipp Emanuel [2]. A strange, rather childlike hand, which C. Freyse assumed to be that of Johann Gottfried Bernhard[7], then continued the entry of names [3–8]:

[1]   Willhelm: Friedeman Bach.
[2]   Carl. Phillipp. Emanuel. Bach.
[3]   Johann. Gottfried. Bernhard: Bach
[4]   Christina: Sophia: Henrietta: Bachin
        mortua est, die 29 junio: aeta[tis]
                                    3 ¼. 1726
[5]   ~~Joh.~~ Gottfried. Heinrich Bach
[6]   Christin²a¹. Gottlieb Bach
[7]   Johann: Sebastian. Bach
[8]   Friedelena Marg[aretha Bach]

Die am Schluss mitgeteilten Namen betreffen zwei erwachsene Familienangehörige, Johann Sebastian Bach [7] und seine Schwägerin Friedelena Margaretha Bach (1675–1729) [8], ältere Schwester der ersten Ehefrau Maria Barbara. Sie lebte, wie schon berichtet wurde, seit den frühen Zeiten der jungen Familie in Weimar, wohl seit 1709, im Familienverbund und starb am 28. Juli 1729 in Leipzig in der Kantorenwohnung am Thomaskirchhof.[8] Alle anderen Namen nennen in der Reihenfolge ihrer Geburt die zu diesem Zeitpunkt lebenden Kinder erster – mit Ausnahme der ältesten Schwester Catharina Dorothea – und zweiter Ehe Bachs. Nach dem Namen unter der Ziffer [3], dem sechsten Kind erster Ehe [9], folgt unter [4] jenes erstgeborene Kind zweiter Ehe, dessen Geburtseintrag sich bisher in keinem Taufregister auffinden lässt, das aber in Leipzig als kleines Mädchen von 3 Jahren und drei Monaten verstarb. Das hier genannte Todesdatum ist identisch mit dem des Leipziger Ratsleichenbuches.[10] Unter [5] ist der erste Sohn zweiter Ehe eingetragen, dessen Namen irrtümlich die Abkürzung für Johann beigegeben und wieder gestrichen wurde (vgl. Taufzettel 1). Dann folgt der zweite Sohn zweiter Ehe [6], dessen ersten Vornamen der Schreiber – Umstellung zweier Buchstaben durch Nummerierung – korrigieren musste; er wird im jungen Alter von 3 Jahren und fünf Monaten im September 1728 sterben (vgl. Taufzettel 2).

The two last names refer to the two adult family members, Johann Sebastian Bach [7] and his sister-in-law Friedelena Margaretha Bach (1675–1729) [8], the older sister of his first wife Maria Barbara. As mentioned earlier, she had lived with the young family since the early times in Weimar, presumably since 1709, and died in Leipzig on July 28, 1729 in the cantor's apartment in Thomaskirchhof.[8] All the other names are recorded in the order of their births and refer to the children of Bach's first marriage still living at that time – with the exception of the oldest sister Catharina Dorothea – and to those of his second marriage. The name of no. [3], the sixth child from the first marriage[9], was followed under [4] by that of the firstborn child from the second marriage, whose baptismal record has not been found in any parish register, but who died in Leipzig as a little girl aged three years and three months. The date of daeath given is identical with that one of the Leipzig death register.[10] Registered as no. [5] is the first son of Bach's second marriage, to whose name was mistakenly added the abbreviated form of Johann and then crossed out again (see baptismal slip 1). Then followed the second son from the second marriage [6] whose first Christian name the writer had to correct by exchanging two letters using numbers; this boy died in September 1728 at

Den ältesten Sohn Johann Sebastian Bachs sehen wir aufgrund der hinzugezogenen Zeugnisse aus seinen Schulheften als Schüler der Thomasschule vornehmlich mit Arbeiten seiner sprachlichen und religiösen Ausbildung beschäftigt. In beiden Heften handelt es sich um Eintragungen aus den Jahren 1726 und 1727, z.T. von unterschiedlicher Hand. Während das Gedicht zweifelsfrei Wilhelm Friedemann zuzuweisen ist, ist es die Namensliste mit der Eintragung seines und seines Bruders Namen nur vermutlich. Überraschung mag zunächst allerdings die Konfrontation mit dem Todesgedanken in beiden Fällen bereiten, öffnet aber einen Zug des Charakters des ältesten Bachsohnes, den man als durchaus typisch erkennen mag.

Sollte zutreffen, was vermutet wurde, hätten wir in der Fortsetzung der zitierten Namensliste die Handschrift des sechsten Kindes erster Ehe vor uns, des am 11. Mai 1715 in Weimar geborenen **Johann Gottfried Bernhard** (1715–1739). Die für ihn in Anspruch genommene Handschrift wäre die des Zehnjährigen. Gleich seinen Brüdern Wilhelm Friedemann und Carl Philipp Emanuel besuchte er in Leipzig die Thomasschule als Externer, erhielt musikalischen Unterricht bei seinem Vater und gehörte ebenso zu den verlässlichen Stützen seines Vaters bei der Herstellung von Aufführungsmaterialien zur Leipziger Kirchenmusik. Ähnlich wie für Wilhelm

the tender age of three years and five months (see baptismal slip no. 2). From the above-discussed references in his notebooks it appears that Johann Sebastian Bach's oldest son in his time at the Thomasschule principally was occupied with studying languages and religion. The entries in the two notebooks were written in the years 1726 and 1727 by different hands. While the poem can doubtlessly be assigned to Wilhelm Friedemann, the same cannot be said about the family list with his and his brothers' names. Still, in both instances the preoccupation with the reality of death may at first surprise. Yet in fact this gives us a glimpse of the disposition of Bach's oldest son which may be recognized as quite typical.

As has been suggested, the hand continuing the roster of family members may well be that of the sixth child of the first marriage, **Johann Gottfried Bernhard** (1715–1739), who was born in Weimar on May 11, 1715. This would mean that the hand displayed in the notebook is that of the ten-year-old boy. Like his brothers Wilhelm Friedemann and Carl Philipp Emanuel, Johann Gottfried Bernhard attended the St. Thomas School as a non-boarding pupil, received music lessons from his father, and was a dependable helpmate in preparing performance material for the Leipzig church music. As for Wilhelm Friedemann – but not for Carl Philipp

Friedemann – nicht so für Carl Philipp Emanuel – setzte sich sein Vater aktiv bei der Suche geeigneter beruflicher Stellen ein, so mit mehreren Empfehlungsschreiben an Mitglieder des Mühlhäuser Stadtrates im Jahr 1735. Nur knapp 1½ Jahre später empfiehlt Johann Sebastian Bach seinen Sohn erneut, diesmal für die Neubesetzung der Stelle des Stadt- und Figuralorganisten in Sangerhausen, St. Jacobi und St. Ulrici. Hier knüpfte er an seine eigene Bewerbung von 1702 an. Der Sohn wird angestellt, doch nach einem knappen Jahr im März 1738 verlässt er Sangerhausen ebenso fluchtartig wie einst Mühlhausen. Lange Monate des Bangens und Wartens folgen. Nach dem 27. Mai 1739 erfährt sein Vater vom Tod seines Sohnes: er sei in Jena am hitzigen Fieber gestorben. Ein wehmütiger Brief Bachs stammt vom Pfingstsonnabend 1738. Dort schreibt er abschließend:

Waß soll ich mehr sagen oder thun? Da keine Vermahnung, ja gar keine liebreiche Vorsorge und *assistence* [Unterstützung] mehr zureichen will, so muß mein Creütz in Geduld tragen, meinen ungerathenen Sohn aber lediglich Göttlicher Barmhertzigkeit überlaßen, nicht zweifelnd, Dieselbe werde mein wehmüthiges Flehen erhören, und endlich nach seinem heiligen Willen an selbigem arbeiten, daß er lerne erkennen, wie die Bekehrung einig und allein Göttlicher Güte zuzuschreiben.[11]

Emanuel – his father was actively engaged in finding suitable professional positions for him, for example writing several letters of recommendation to the members of the Mühlhausen town council in 1735. Barely a year and a half later Johann Sebastian Bach recommended his son again, this time as successor of the organist at St. Jacobi and St. Ulrici in Sangerhausen. In 1702 Bach had himself applied for that position. His son's application was successful, but in March 1738 he left Sangerhausen after having been there little less than a year, leaving as hastily as he had left Mühlhausen. Months of worrying and waiting followed. After May 27, 1739, J. S. Bach heard about his son's death; evidently he had died in Jena of a fever. In a melancholy letter dated the day before Whitsun 1738 Bach had concluded:

"What more shall I say or do? Since no rebuke, or indeed affectionate precaution and assistance will achieve anything more, I must bear my cross in patience and leave my undutiful son to divine mercy, not doubting that God will hear my distressing cries and eventually work out his holy will, so that he learns to recognize that salvation comes solely from divine grace."[11]

In commenting directly on Johann Gottfried Bernhard in our survey of the children of Bach's first marriage, we have skipped no less than three of Bach's offspring. After the

In der Reihenfolge der Kinder Bachs aus erster Ehe haben wir mit dem sofortigen Bezug zu Johann Gottfried Bernhard nicht weniger als drei weitere Kinder übersprungen; denn nach der Geburt eines Zwillingspärchens am 23. Februar 1713 in Abwesenheit Johann Sebastians – **Maria Sophia** stirbt nach drei Wochen, **Johann Christoph** noch am gleichen Tag [12] – wird als fünftes Kind erster Ehe **Carl Philipp Emanuel** (1714–1788) am 8. März 1714 in Weimar geboren. In Vielem gestaltet sich das Leben seiner Kinder- und Jugendzeit ähnlich dem seines älteren Bruders. Sein Vater ließ ihn, ähnlich wie schon zuvor Wilhelm Friedemann, für das Studium an der Juristenfakultät der Leipziger Universität vormerken; das Studium begann er 1731 in Leipzig und setzte es 1734 in Frankfurt/Oder fort. Nach Abschluss des Studiums 1738 lebte er in Berlin und in Hamburg. Sachsen schien lediglich nach dem Tod des Nachfolgers seines Vaters in Leipzig, Gottlob Harrer (1703–1755), nochmals als Ziel seiner Wünsche in Betracht zu kommen, als er sich als Thomaskantor bewarb, aber gegenüber Johann Friedrich Doles (1715–1797) unterlag.

Dreieinhalb Jahre nach Johann Gottfried Bernhards Geburt hatte sich wieder Nachwuchs bei der inzwischen in Köthen lebenden Bachfamilie angemeldet: Am 15. November 1718 wird Maria Barbara von einem Sohn entbunden; es ist das siebente Kind – fünfter Sohn – der ersten Ehe Bachs.

birth of twins on February 23, 1713 in Johann Sebastian's absence – **Maria Sophia** died after three weeks, **Johann Christoph** still on the same day [12] **Carl Philipp Emanuel** (1714–1788) was born on March 8, 1714 in Weimar as the fifth child of the first marriage. In many respects, his childhood and adolescence were similar to those of his older brother. His father secured for him a place of study at the law school of Leipzig university, as he had done earlier for Wilhelm Friedemann; Carl Philipp began his studies in 1731 at Leipzig and continued them in 1734 at Frankfurt/Oder. After receiving his degree in 1738, he lived in Berlin and Hamburg. It appears that after the death of Gottlob Harrer (1703–1755), his father's successor in Leipzig, Saxony became the object of his aspirations only once more when he applied for the position of cantor of St. Thomas but was rejected in favor of Johann Friedrich Doles (1715–1797).

Three and a half years after Johann Gottfried Bernhard's birth, there was another addition to the Bach family now living in Köthen: On November 15, 1718, Maria Barbara gave birth to a son. This was the seventh child – and the fifth son – of Bach's first marriage. Two days later the infant was baptized in the chapel of Köthen castle and was named **Leopold August**. But the parents could not enjoy him for long: The little boy died after ten

Zwei Tage später wird dieser in der Köthener Schlosskirche getauft und erhält den Namen **Leopold August**. Doch die Eltern konnten sich dieses Kindes nicht lange erfreuen. Bereits nach zehn Monaten verstarb der kleine Knabe; er wurde am 28. September 1719 auf dem Köthener Friedhof beigesetzt. Und ebenfalls nur knapp zehn Monate später verstarb Bachs erste Ehefrau Maria Barbara. Bach erfuhr erst von ihrem Tod und dem Begräbnis, als er von einer Kurreise mit seinem Fürsten aus Karlsbad zurückkehrte.

months and on September 28, 1719, was buried in the Köthen cemetery. And only ten months later Bach's first wife Maria Barbara died as well. Bach learned of her death and funeral only upon returning with employer from a journey to the spa in Karlsbad.

Von Bachs Kindern aus der zweiten Ehe und ihrem Lebensweg

Von **Christiana Sophia Henrietta** (1723–1726), der ersten Tochter und zugleich erstem Kind der Ehe Bachs mit Anna Magdalena war schon gesprochen worden. Sie muss in der zweiten Märzhälfte 1723 geboren worden sein. Das jedenfalls lässt die etwas pauschale Altersangabe von 3 ¼ Jahren, die wir aus dem Schulheft Wilhelm Friedemanns kennen und den drei Jahren, die das Totenbuch der Stadt Leipzig vom 29. Juni 1726 nennt, errechnen: „Ein Mägdlein 3. Jahr, Christiana Sophia *Henrietta*, Herrn Johann Sebastian Bachs, *Cantoris* bey der *Thomas* Schule, am *Thomas* Kirchhofe, st[arb]. Sonnabend [30.6.1726]."[13] Die Familie befand sich noch in Köthen. Da jedoch dort kein Taufeintrag nachweisbar ist, muss angenommen werden, dass

The Children of Bach's Second Marriage

Christiana Sophia Henrietta (1723–1726), the first child of Bach's marriage with Anna Magdalena, has already been mentioned. She must have been born in the second half of March, 1723, an assumption based on Wilhelm Friedemann's notebook entry, which speaks of an age of 3 ¼ years, and on the Leipzig register of deaths which has the following entry on June 29, 1726:
"A little girl, in her 3rd year, Christiana Sophia Henrietta, daughter of Johann Sebastian Bach, cantor of the St. Thomas School, in Thomaskirchhof, died Saturday [June 30, 1726]."[13] The Bach family was still in Köthen at that time. Since there is no record of a baptism, it must be assumed that Anna Magdalena had given birth somewhere else. Perhaps she stayed

Anna Magdalena dieses Mädchens an einem anderen Ort zur Welt gebracht hatte. Möglich erscheint ein Aufenthalt bei ihren Eltern in Weißenfels; denkbar ist auch ein Aufenthalt bei der Familie ihres Bruders in Zerbst. Völlig unaufklärbar wären ganz andere Möglichkeiten. Der Vorname „Henrietta" legt allerdings – wie bei dem letzten Kind erster Ehe – Patenschaften aus dem Umkreis des Köthener Hofes nahe, denkt man an die junge Köthener Serenissima, Friederica Henrietta (1702–1723), die wenige Tage nach der Geburt des Bachschen Kindes am 4. April starb. Der aufwendige Umzug der Familie von Köthen nach Leipzig fiel jedenfalls in die Zeit des gerade beendeten zweiten Lebensmonats ihres kleinsten Kindes. Von dem Ereignis berichtete die „Stats- u. Gelehrte Zeitung Des Hollsteinischen unpartheyischen Correspondenten":
> Am vergangenen Sonnabend zu Mittage kamen 4. Wagen mit Haus-Raht beladen von Cöthen allhier an, so dem gewesenen dasigen Fürstl. Capell-Meister, als nach Leipzig vocirten Cantori Figurali, zugehöreten; Um 2. Uhr kam er selbst nebst seiner Familie auf 2 Kutschen an, und bezog die in der Thomas-Schule neu renovirte Wohnung. [14]

Diese Meldung der Ausgabe Nummer 89 vom 4. Juni war mit dem Datum des 29. Mai versehen und bezog sich auf den 22. Mai, den Sonnabend nach Pfingsten. In den dem Hausrat nachfolgenden zwei

with her parents in Weißenfels or with her brother's family in Zerbst. Other possibilities are rather implausible. The Christian name "Henrietta" implies, however, that – as with the last child of Bach's first marriage – the godparents came from the circles of the court in Köthen, considering the name of the young princess of Köthen, Friederica Henrietta (1702–1723), who died only a few days after the birth of Bach's child on April 4. In any case, the arduous move of the family from Köthen to Leipzig took place when the youngest child was just about two months old. There is a notice on the move in the "Stats- u. Gelehrte Zeitung Des Hollsteinischen unpartheyischen Correspondenten":
> "This past Saturday at noon, four wagons loaded with household goods arrived here from Cöthen; they belonged to the former Princely Capellmeister there now called to Leipzig as *Cantor Figuralis*. He himself arrived with his family on 2 carriages at 2 o'clock and moved into the newly renovated apartment in the St. Thomas School." [14]

This notice, published in no. 89 on June 4, was dated May 29 and referred to May 22, the Saturday after Whitsunday. In the two carriages that followed the wagons with household goods was the family of eight: Anna Magdalena and Sebastian Bach, his sister-in-law Friedelena Margaretha, the children Catharina Dorothea, Wilhelm

Kutschen befanden sich die achtköpfige Familie, das Ehepaar Bach, die Schwägerin Friedelena Margaretha, die Kinder Catharina Dorothea, Wilhelm Friedemann, Carl Philipp Emanuel, Johann Gottfried Bernhard und die neugeborene Christiana Sophia Henrietta. Neun Monate später sollten die Kinder ein weiteres Geschwisterkind erhalten.

Taufzettel 1
Mit **Gottfried Heinrich** (1724–1763) wenden wir uns dem erstgeborenen Sohn und zweitem Kind zweiter Ehe zu. Zugleich wird mit seiner Geburt die Reihe der Bachschen Taufzettel in der Thomaskirche zu Leipzig eröffnet. Er wurde am 26. Februar 1724 in Leipzig geboren und am Tag darauf, dem Sonntag Invocavit, erstem Sonntag der Passionszeit, getauft. Die Nummerierung der Registrierzeilen des Taufzettels (Zeilen 15–17) weist auf die 32. Taufe im Monat Februar und die 72. Taufe in der Thomaskirche im Jahr 1724 hin. Der Vermerk „☉. *H. L. S.*" nennt den Wochentag, Sonntag, und den Namen des Taufpfarrers durch Kürzel; es handelt sich um den Diaconus Lic. Urban Gottfried Sieber (1669–1741), der den sogenannten Wöchnerdienst zu versehen hatte, also zuständig war für die in dieser Woche anfallenden Kasualdienste. Sieber war ein gelehrter Herr; für ihn erstritt die Theologische Fakultät der Universität im Jahr 1715 eine außerordentliche Professur für Kirchengeschichte, was zu dieser Zeit

Friedemann, Carl Philipp Emanuel and Johann Gottfried Bernhard, and the infant Christiana Sophia Henrietta. Nine months later the children would welcome another sibling.

Baptismal slip 1
With **Gottfried Heinrich** (1724–1763) we turn our attention to the first son and second child of Bach's second marriage. The record of his birth is found at the beginning of the set of baptismal slips relating to the Bach family at St. Thomas. Gottfried was born in Leipzig on February 26, 1724 and was baptized the following day, Invocavit Sunday, the first Sunday of Lent. The numbers in the registration lines of the baptismal slip (lines 15–17) convey that this was the 32nd baptism in February and the 72nd baptism of the year 1724 at St. Thomas. The annotation "☉. *H. L. S.*" indicates the day of the week, Sunday, and the abbreviated name of the officiating pastor: Deacon Lic. Urban Gottfried Sieber (1669–1741), who was responsible that week for casual services. Sieber was highly educated. In 1715 the university's faculty of theology gained for him a lecturership in church history, which was considered a great exception at the time. If the baptismal service did not take place at midday between 11 and

Lic. Urban Gottfried Sieber (1669–1741), Pfarrer der Thomaskirche

Lic. Urban Gottfried Sieber (1669–1741), pastor of the St. Thomas Church

als ausgesprochene Ausnahme galt. Wenn der Taufgottesdienst, den er hielt, nicht in der Mittagszeit zwischen 11 und 13 Uhr stattgefunden hat, könnte er nur noch am späteren Nachmittag gefeiert worden sein, denn als Diaconus hatte Sieber auch den Vespergottesdienst zwischen 13.30 und 15 Uhr zu halten. Zusammen mit dem Kind Bachs wurden offenbar zwei weitere Kinder getauft, deren Namen auf der Rückseite neben dem Namen Gottfried Heinrichs verzeichnet sind: Susanna Elisabeth und Johanna Susanna. Der Taufzettel ist von einem Schreiber wie ein Formular vorbereitet worden, zeigt aber deutlich Johann Sebastians eigene Schrift bei seinem Namen, seinen Titeln, dem Namen seiner Frau und dem Kindesnamen (Zeilen 2–5).

1:00 o'clock, it can only have been celebrated in the late afternoon because his responsibilities as deacon required Sieber also to conduct the vesper service between 1:30 and 3 o'clock. Apparently two other infants were baptized together with Bach's baby. Their names were recorded on the reverse side of the slip next to that of Gottfried Heinrich: Susanna Elisabeth and Johanna Susanna. The baptismal slip was prepared by a writer in the standard format, but included in Johann Sebastian Bach's own hand his name, his titles, his wife's name, and the name of the child (lines 2–5).

[1]
Zu St: Thomas den 27. Febr: 1724.
Vater ist Herr Johann Sebastian Bach, Director
Musices u. Cantor ad Sch: Thom:
Deßen Eheliebste Frau Anna Magdalena *gebohrne* Wülckin
Kindes Nahme Gottfried Heinrich.

Pathen.
1.) *Herr HoffRath D. Gottfried Lange, Burge-*
Meister alhier.

2) *Frau Regina Maria HEr. M. Johann Heinrich*
Ernesti P. P. P. und der Schulen zu
St: Thomae etc. Rectoris Frau EheLiebste.

3) *Herr D. Friedrich Heinrich Graff, des Ober-*
Hoffgerichts alhier Advocatus Ordinarius.

No $\dfrac{32}{72}$.⊙ *H. L. S.*

[1]
At St. Thomas on February 27, 1724.
The Father is Mr Johann Sebastian Bach, Director
Of Music and Cantor at the St. Thomas School:
His dearest wife Anna Magdalena, *nee* Wülckin
The Child's Name is Gottfried Heinrich.

Godparents
1.) *Court councillor D. Gottfried Lange,*
mayor of Leipzig.

2) *Regina Maria, dearest wife of M. Johann Heinrich*
Ernesti, rector of
the *St. Thomas School.*

3) *Dr. Friedrich Heinrich Graff,*
Attorney at the supreme court in Leipzig.

No $\dfrac{32}{72}$.⊙ *H. L. S.*

Gottfried Lange (1672–1748),
Bürgermeister Leipzigs,
Kirchenvorsteher der Thomaskirche

Gottfried Lange (1672–1748),
major of Leipzig, churchwarden
at St. Thomas

Die Auswahl der Paten weist in drei Richtungen, in die des Stadtrates, der Schule und der Nachbarschaft. Namen gebender Pate ist der regierende Bürgermeister Gottfried Lange (1672–1748).

Gottfried Lange war als Pfarrerssohn in Schwerta bei Greiffenberg/schlesische Oberlausitz geboren worden, hatte nach schulischer Bildung in Niederwiesa bei Greiffenberg und dem Gymnasium zu Zittau im Jahr 1689 in Leipzig das Universitätsstudium zunächst der Theologie, dann der Jurisprudenz aufgenommen und war 1692 Magister geworden. In Erfurt erwarb er 1702 den Doktortitel der

The choice of the godparents points in three directions: the town council, the school of St. Thomas and the neighborhood. The godparent providing the infant's name was the Leipzig mayor Gottfried Lange (1672–1748).

Lange was born in Schwerta near Greiffenberg in the Silesian part of Upper Lusatia as the son of a pastor. After early schooling in Niederwiesa near Greiffenberg and secondary school in Zittau he began his university studies in Leipzig in 1689. He first studied theology, then jurisprudence, and received his master's degree in 1692. In 1702 he acquired his legal doctorate at Erfurt uni-

Rechtswissenschaften. Von August dem Starken gefördert und protegiert, trat er 1710 als Ratsherr in den Leipziger Stadtrat ein; bereits 1719 wurde er zu einem der drei Bürgermeister gewählt. Zwei Neffen – Söhne seiner Schwester –, die z.T. auch in unmittelbarer Nähe Bachs wirkten, konnten sich in Leipzig seiner besonderen Förderung erfreuen: M. Gottlob Schröer (1690–1738), von 1729 an Kollaborator an der Thomasschule, später Sextus der Nikolaischule, und M. Christoph Schröer (1694–1737), der ab 1727 Pfarrer in Eutritzsch war. Zur Thomaskirche trat Lange in eine engere Beziehung durch Ausübung des Kirchenvorsteheramtes.

Als zweite Patin fungierte die Ehefrau des inzwischen alt gewordenen Thomasschulrektors Johann Heinrich Ernesti (1652–1729), Regina Maria, geborene Carpzov (1676–1749).

Regina Maria Ernesti war als Tochter jenes Theologieprofessors Johann Benedict Carpzov (1639–1699) in Leipzig aufgewachsen, der einst mit dem zweiten Amtsvorgänger Bachs Johann Schelle (1648–1701) einig geworden war, Liedpredigten zu eigens von Schelle komponierten Choralkantaten zu halten. Das war 1689 geschehen und mochte ihr, die damals 13 Jahre alt war, noch gut in Erinnerung geblieben sein. Sie hatte selbst 6 Kinder zur Welt gebracht, von denen zwei Töchter noch am Leben waren. 1729 wird sie anlässversity. Sponsored and promoted by August the Strong, he became a member of the Leipzig town council in 1710 and in 1719 was elected one of three mayors. Two nephews – sons of his sister – who also worked partly in the immediate proximity of Bach, enjoyed his special support in Leipzig: M. Gottlob Schröer, (1690–1738), who from 1729 was affiliated with the St. Thomas School and later became *Sextus* of the Nikolai school, and M. Christoph Schröer (1694–1737), who was a parish priest in Eutritzsch from 1727. Lange became closely associated with St. Thomas through his office as churchwarden.

Regina Maria Ernesti, née Carpzov (1676–1749), acted as second godparent. She was the wife of the old rector of the St. Thomas School, Johann Heinrich Ernesti (1652–1729).

Regina Maria Ernesti had grown up in Leipzig. She was the daughter of the professor of theology Johann Benedict Carpzov (1639–1699), who had collaborated with Bach's second predecessor, Johann Schelle (1648–1701), delivering sermons on hymn texts used in chorale cantatas composed by Schelle especially for these occasions. This was in 1689, when Regina Maria was 13 years old; she therefore may well have retained these occasions in her memory. She herself had given birth to six children, of whom two daughters were still alive. In 1729 she heard the performance of Bach's

lich der feierlichen Gedächtnispredigt, die Thomaspastor Christian Weise (1671–1736) ihrem Mann am 21. Oktober in der Universitätskirche St. Pauli hielt, die Aufführung der Begräbnismotette Bachs erleben („Der Geist hilft unser Schwachheit auf" – BWV 226). Ihr Vetter Johann Gottlob Carpzov (1679–1767) wirkte von 1708 als Diaconus, seit 1714 als Archidiaconus an der Thomaskirche, bevor er 1730 als Superintendent nach Lübeck ging. Er ist Taufpfarrer zweier Kindern Bachs, des Ernestus Andreas von 1727 (Taufzettel 4) und der Christiana Louisa Benedicta 1729/1730 (Taufzettel 6).

Der dritte Pate war D. Friedrich Heinrich Graff d. Ä. (1688–1731), der im Blick auf seine späteren familiären Verflechtungen in der Nachbarschaft – Familie Bose – gut mit der Bachfamilie in Verbindung zu bringen ist, zu diesem frühen Zeitpunkt aber Rätsel aufgibt.

Graff hatte eine gute Stellung als *Advocatus Ordinarius* am Oberhofgericht in Leipzig. Er war verheiratet mit Johanna Dorothea, geborene Rivinus, (1696–1780), einer Schwester der beiden Juristen Prof. Dr. Johann Florens Rivinus (1681–1755) und D. Andreas Florens Rivinus (1701–1761). Der letztgenannte Andreas Florens Rivinus taucht als Pate bei Bachs 1727 geborenem Sohn Ernestus Andreas auf (vgl. Taufzettel 4). Der erstgenannte Rivinus wird Empfänger der Huldigungskantate „Die Freude reget sich,

funeral motet "Der Geist hilft unser Schwachheit auf" BWV 226 on the occasion of a solemn memorial sermon preached by the pastor of St. Thomas, Christian Weise (1671–1736) in the University Church of St. Paul on October 21 during a memorial service for her husband. Her cousin Johann Gottlob Carpzov (1679–1767) in 1708 became a deacon of St. Thomas and in 1714 advanced to the position of archdeacon; in 1730 he moved to Lübeck, where he was made superintendent. He baptized two of Bach's children, Ernestus Andreas (1727, baptismal slip no. 4) and Christiana Louisa Benedicta (1729/1730, baptism slip no. 6).

The third godparent was D. Friedrich Heinrich Graff the older (1688–1731), who later had many connections with the Bach family through near-by relatives – the Bose family. There are some enigmas about his early years.

Graff held a splendid position as *Advocatus Ordinarius*, or chief prosecutor, at the Leipzig supreme court. He was married to Johanna Dorothea, née Rivinus (1696–1780), a sister of the two attorneys Prof. Dr. Johann Florens Rivinus (1681–1755) and D. Andreas Florens Rivinus (1701–1761). Andreas Florens Rivinus later became godparent of Bach's son Ernestus Andreas, who was born in 1727 (see baptismal slip no. 4). His brother Johann Florens was the dedicatee of the cantata "Die Freude

erhebt die muntern Töne" (BWV 36b) sein (vgl. dazu Taufzettel 10). Von Gottfried Heinrichs Musikalität wissen wir verhältnismäßig wenig, und dennoch gehört er zu den musikalischen Bachsöhnen, wahrscheinlich sogar in die allererste Reihe. Und dies, obwohl wir von ihm keine Komposition, nicht eine Note kennen. In der Genealogie der Bachschen Familie, die Johann Sebastian Bach 1735 niederschrieb und die nur durch eine Abschrift der Tochter Carl Philipp Emanuel Bachs erhalten blieb, erfahren wir über ihn: „inclinirt [wendet sich] gleichfalls zur Musik, inspecie [insbesondere] zum Clavier"; und Carl Philipp Emanuel fügte Folgendes hinzu: „War ein großes Genie, welches aber nicht entwickelt ward. Starb 1761 in Leipzig, oder Naumburg".[15]

Zum großen Kummer seiner Eltern litt ihr erster Sohn an einer geistigen Behinderung, deren Ausmaß wir nicht kennen. Die Bemerkungen des Vaters und des Bruders zeigen aber, dass es sich neben dieser Behinderung um eine einseitig hohe musikalische Begabung gehandelt hat, die sich weder systematisch entwickeln noch regelmäßig einsetzen ließ. In der Familie mag man sich an die Schwester des Eisenacher Vaters und Großvaters Johann Ambrosius Bach erinnert haben, Dorothea Maria Bach, die im Eisenacher Hause bis zu ihrem Tod am 6. Februar 1679 verblieben war. Auch sie war durch eine geistige Behinderung nicht

regt sich, erhebt die munteren Töne" BWV 36b cf. baptismal slip no. 10). While we know little about Gottfried Heinrich's musicality, he clearly counted among Bach's musically talented sons. And this even though we have no composition, indeed not a single note of him. In the genealogy of Bach's family, written down by Johann Sebastian Bach in 1735 and preserved in a single copy by the daughter of Carl Philipp Emanuel Bach we learn about Johann Gottfried: "He is also inclined towards music, especially the keyboard," to which Carl Philipp Emanuel added: "A great genius who, however, did not mature. He died in Leipzig or Naumburg in 1761."[15]

To the deep sorrow of his parents their oldest son suffered from a mental disability whose nature we do not exactly know. The remarks of his father and his brother show, however, that despite his disability he possessed great musical gifts, which could, however, neither be systematically developed nor regularly employed. His case might have reminded his family of Dorothea Maria Bach, the sister of Johann Ambrosius, who lived in the Eisenach family home until her death on February 6, 1679. She, too, due to a mental disorder could not profit from regular education and was dependent on her family for her entire life. And Gottfried Heinrich, too, of whom we hear again only on

35

bildungsfähig gewesen und blieb ihr Leben lang unselbständig. Auch Gottfried Heinrich, von dem wir erst wieder anlässlich der Erbteilung nach dem Tod des Vaters hören, war auf solche Betreuung in der Familie angewiesen. Aus Briefen des bereits genannten Schweinfurter Vetters Bachs, Johann Elias Bach (1705–1755), erfahren wir, dass dieser als Hauslehrer im April 1739 dabei war, die „beyden ältesten Untergebenen", d. h. Gottfried Heinrich und Elisabeth Juliana Friederica (vgl. Taufzettel 3), „zum Tisch des Herrn [zu] praepariren".[16] Offenbar hatte man bei Gottfried Heinrich wegen seiner Behinderung noch ein wenig mit der Vorbereitung auf die erste Abendmahlsteilnahme gewartet und ließ diese jetzt zusammen mit der zwei Jahre jüngeren Schwester vollziehen.

Gottfried Heinrich war mit der Mutter Anna Magdalena, den zwei kleinen Schwestern Johanna Carolina (1737–1781) und Regina Susanna (1742–1809), dem fünfzehnjährigen Johann Christian (1735–1782) und der sehr viel älteren Halbschwester Catharina Dorothea (1708–1774) anwesend als der Vater starb. Am Ende des Jahres 1750 verzeichnete das Kommunikantenregister der Leipziger Thomaskirche „Mr: Bach u Bruder", womit wohl Wilhelm Friedemann und Gottfried Heinrich gemeint sind. Zehn Jahre später, nach dem Tod der Mutter, nahm ihn seine jüngere Schwester Elisabeth Juliana

the occasion of the settlement of his father's estate, was dependent on such family support.

From letters of Bach's Schweinfurt cousin Johann Elias Bach (1705–1755), who has already been mentioned, we learn that in April 1739 he was engaged as private tutor in "preparing the two oldest", i. e. Gottfried Heinrich and Elisabeth Juliana Friederica (see baptismal slip no. 3), "for the Lord's Supper."[16] Apparently it had been decided that due to his handicap Gottfried Heinrich should wait a little and then take his first "Lord's Supper" together with his younger sister. When his father died, Gottfried Heinrich was present together with his mother Anna Magdalena, his two youngest sisters Johanna Carolina (1737–1781) and Regina Susanna (1742–1809), the fifteen-year-old Johann Christian (1735–1782), and his much older half-sister Dorothea (1708–1774). At the end of 1750 the communicant register of St. Thomas in Leipzig recorded "Mr. Bach and brother", apparently referring to Wilhelm Friedemann and Gottfried Heinrich. Ten years later, after the death of their mother, his younger sister Elisabeth Juliana Friederica Altnickol (1726–1781) took him to Naumburg (see baptismal slip no. 3). From the library of his father he received, among other books, the detailed *Erklärung der Bibel*, the biblical commentary of Johann Ole-

*Johann Olearius, Biblische Erklärung, Bd. 1,
Leipzig 1679: Porträt*

*Johann Olearius, Biblical Commentary,
Vol. 1, Leipzig, 1679. Portrait*

Friederica Altnickol (1726–1781) zu sich nach Naumburg (vgl. Taufzettel 3). Aus dem theologischen Buchbestand seines Vaters erhielt er aufgrund des Loswurfs unter anderen Bänden die umfangreiche „Biblische Erklärung" von Johann Olearius, fünf Bände in folio (Leipzig 1679–1681), die für das Verständnis des geistlichen Vokalwerks Bachs von größter Bedeutung ist. Womöglich ist dieses wichtige Werk aus Johann Sebastian Bachs theologischem Buchbestand danach in den Besitz der betreuenden Schwester oder anderer Personen in Naumburg gelangt.
Am 12. Februar 1763 ist Gottfried Heinrich in Naumburg beigesetzt worden.

arius published in five folio volumes (Leipzig 1679–1681), which is of great importance for the understanding of Bach's sacred vocal works. These important volumes from Johann Sebastian Bach's theological library later probably came into the possession of his sister or other persons in Naumburg. Gottfried Heinrich was buried in Naumburg on February 12, 1763.

Taufzettel 2

Knapp zwei Wochen nach Ostern 1725, wohl am Freitag, dem 13. April, kommt das dritte Kind in Bachs zweiter Ehe zur Welt. Es ist ein Junge, der sogleich am folgenden Sonnabend, dem 14. April 1725 in der Thomaskirche getauft wird (18–20). Die ausgeschriebene, aber doch recht eigentümliche Handschrift dieses Taufzettels fällt gegenüber allen anderen etwas aus dem Rahmen; Bach selbst trägt den Namen seines Sohnes ein: **Christian Gottlieb** (1725–1728). Eine dritte Handschrift vermerkt eine stellvertretende Person für die erstgenannte Patin, verbessert nächst der laufenden Ziffer der Taufen im Monat April 1725 – die 22. – die laufende Ziffer für die 140. Taufe (aus Ziffer 139) im Jahr 1725, was auch auf der Rückseite des Zettels zu bemerken ist; daneben folgt der Vermerk zum Tauftag und zum Taufpfarrer: *♄ H. M. R.*, was auf Sonnabend hinweist und M. Justus Gotthard Rabener (1688–1731) als Taufpfarrer nennt, seit 1721 Subdiaconus an der Thomaskirche. Dieser hatte zuvor Stellen an der Peterskirche, der Thomaskirche und an der Neuen Kirche innegehabt. Wenige Monate vor seinem Tod im August 1731 wurde er an der Thomaskirche zum Diaconus befördert. Mit Rabener, der noch für weitere drei Kinder Bachs als Taufpfarrer tätig gewesen ist (Taufzettel 3, 5 und 7), verbindet sich eine Skandalgeschichte, die kurz angedeutet sei:

Baptismal slip 2

Almost two weeks after Easter 1725, probably on Friday, April 13, the third child of Bach's second marriage was born, a boy. He was baptized on the following Saturday, April 14, 1725 in St. Thomas Church (lines 18–20). The baptismal slip was filled out in a rather unusual hand, differing significantly from the other slips. Bach himself entered his son's name: **Christian Gottlieb** (1725–1728). A third hand made a note of the representative for the first godparent and next to the current number of baptisms that month – the 22nd – corrected that of the year, i.e. the 140th (not 139th) in 1725; this can also be seen on the reverse side of the slip. Next comes the day of the week the baptism took place and the name of the officiating clergy: "♄ H. M. R.", which suggests a Saturday and M. Justus Gotthard Rabener, (1688–1731), as the officiating pastor. Rabener had served as assistant deacon at St. Thomas since 1721, having previously held positions at St. Peter's, St. Thomas, and the Neue Kirche. A few months before his death in August, 1731, he was made deacon of St. Thomas. Rabener, who acted as officiating pastor for three more of Bach's children (baptismal slips nos. 3, 5 and 7), is connected with a scandalous story, which will be briefly related:

Im Anschluss an eigene Unterrichtung beauftragte im Jahr 1703 sein Vater, Joachim Gotthart Rabener, einst Leipziger Schöppen- und Gerichtsschreiber, M. Adam Bernd (1676–1748), ihn privat auf das Universitätsstudium vorbereiten. Bernd muss zu dieser Zeit als Persönlichkeit von ungewöhnlicher geistiger und geistlicher Begabung gegolten haben. Seine Predigt- und Einflusskraft muss von erstaunlicher Wirkung gewesen sein. Deshalb verwundert es nicht, wenn ihn der Stadtrat im Jahr 1711 als Oberkatecheten an der neu eröffneten Peterskirche anstellte. Er habe „viel Beyfall im Predigen" gehabt, „oft hielten 40 Kutschen nach der Predigt vor der Kirchenthüre, und die Vornehmsten der Stadt waren seine Zuhörer".[17] Das hielt eine Zeitlang an. Als er im Jahr 1728 aber einen Traktat mit dem Titel „Einfluss der göttlichen Wahrheiten in den Willen und in das Leben der Menschen" herausgab, aus dem eine besondere Neigung zur römisch-katholischen Sicht der Rechtfertigung sprach, wurde er suspendiert und schließlich trotz Widerrufs seines Amtes enthoben. Im Herbst 1728 eskalierte die Diskussion um Bernd; auch Rabener meldete sich in scharfen Attacken gegen seinen ehemaligen Lehrer zu Wort. Ohne Aufklärendes zu dem Prozess mitzuteilen, der nach Rabeners Tod gegen diesen geführt wurde, berichtet Bernd 1738 in seiner

His father, Joachim Gotthart Rabener, a Leipzig court clerk, in 1703 engaged M. Adam Bernd, (1676–1748) to prepare Justus privately for the university. At that time Bernd must have been regarded as an individual of uncommon intellectual and religious gifts. The strength of his sermons and his charisma must have been astounding. It therefore came as no surprise when the Leipzig town council employed him in 1711 as first catechist of the newly consecrated church of St. Peter. It was said that "his sermons met with great acclaim" and "often 40 coaches stopped after the sermon in front of the church door, and the most distinguished citizens were in the audience."[17] This lasted for a while. But when in 1728 he published a treatise with the title *Einfluß der göttlichen Wahrheiten in den Willen, und in das gantze Leben des Menschen* ("The Influence of Divine Truths on the Will and the Entire Life of Humankind"), in which he expressed a special affinity to the Roman Catholic view of justification, he was suspended and – despite his revocation – eventually defrocked. The discussion about Bernd escalated in the autumn of 1728; Rabener, too, voiced his opinion in sharp attacks against his former teacher. In 1738, Bernd mentioned in his autobiography the results of such behaviour without

Lebensbeschreibung von den Folgen solchen Verhaltens:
„Seine Erben haben bey seinem Lebens-Lauffe, den sie aufgesetzet, mir die Ehre nicht angethan, daß sie mich unter seine *Praeceptores* [Lehrer] gesetzet hätten; vielleicht weil sie mich unter seinen *Praeceptoribus* nicht gefunden haben; es würde auch vor den Verstorbenen keine große Ehre gewesen seyn. Ungeachtet er mein Schüler gewesen, so war er doch nach der Zeit mein bitterster Feind, welches ich eher nicht, als vor 10. Jahren bey der *Melodianischen Affaire*[18] erfahren. In einem gewissen *Conventu* [Zusammenkunft], da über mich beratschlaget wurde, *harangurte* [tadelnd schwätzen] er die gantze Zeit alleine, und redete auf das hefftigste wider mich, wollte auch von allem gelinden Verfahren wider mich nicht das geringste hören. Das hat ihm aber nach seinem Tode viel geschadet. Denn weil ein gewisser gelehrter Mann, der stets viel Liebe und Hochachtung vor mich gehabt, dadurch erschrecklich erbittert, und aufgebracht wurde, daß niemand so sehr als er, in Gesellschafften die bittersten Reden wider mich ausgestossen; so war er hernach die erste Ursache des Processes, der seinethalben nach seinem Tode geführet wurde, da sonst die gantze Sache wol würde seyn liegen blieben."[19]
Auf der Rückseite des Taufzettels sind von dritter Hand neben dem Namen throwing light on the lawsuit which was brought against Rabener after his death: "In his curriculum vitae, written by his heirs, I am not given the honor of beeing named among his teachers; perhaps they didn't find me among his preceptors, but even so it would not have been a great honor for the deceased. Although he was my pupil, he afterwards was my deadliest enemy, which I did not learn until ten years ago through the *Melodian Affair*.[18] In a certain meeting, in which my case was discussed, he harangued me all the time and argued most intensely, not in the least interested in resolving the issues against me. However, this harmed him much after his death. For a certain educated individual, who had always loved and deeply respected me, was terribly incensed and embittered by the fact that he made the worst public comments about me; later this individual was the initial cause of the law suit against him after his death; otherwise the whole matter would probably have been disregarded."[19]
On the reverse side of the baptismal slip, next to the name of Bach's infant child, Christian Gottlieb, a third hand noted the names of two other children: Johann Jacob, and Johann Franz.

des Bachschen Jungen, Christian Gottlieb, noch zwei weitere Kindesnamen
aufgeschrieben: Johann Jacob und
Johann Franz.

[2] *Tauffzeddul* *Zu St. Thomas*
  ao 1725.
 Das Kind soll heißen *den 14. April*
 Christian, Gottlieb,

  Vater ist
  HErr Johañ Sebastian Bach, Director Musices
  und Cantor Scholae ad div. Thom:

  Mutter.
  Frau Anna Magdalena, gebohrne Wilckin

  Pathen werden seyn
  Frau Maria Elisabeth
   Herrn Johañ Christian Tauberts, Handelsmañs
 st. Fr. Johanna Margretha Eheliebste
 H. Balthas. Heinr. v. Brincks Ehel.

  HErr Christian Wilhelm Ludewig, bey der Königl.
   und Churfürstl. Sachß. GleitsEiñahme bestalter
   Gleitsmañ.

  HErr Gottlieb Christian Wagner, Handelmañ, und
   E.E. Hochw. Raths Güter Bestätiger.

No $\frac{22}{140}$ ♄ H. M. R.

[2]

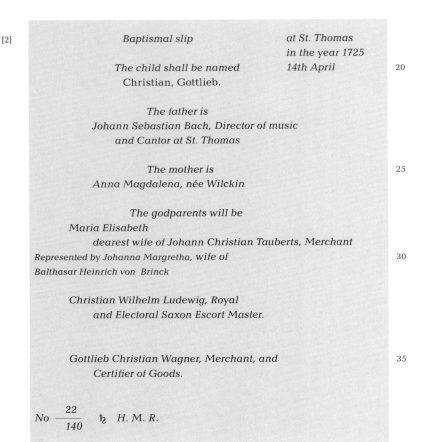

Von der erstgenannten Patin Maria Elisabeth Taubert, geborene Windel (1680–1740), Ehefrau des Kaufmanns Johann Christian Taubert (1672–vor 1740), wissen wir kaum mehr als den Namen. Auf dem Taufzettel steht sie an erster Stelle, während das Taufbuch

We know hardly more than the name of the first godparent Maria Elisabeth Taubert, née Windel (1680–1740), the wife of the merchant Johann Christian Taubert (1672 – before 1740). On the baptismal slip her name is the first to be mentioned, while the baptismal

sie an zweite Stelle rückt, wohl weil sie verhindert war an der Taufe teilzunehmen. Deshalb wurde sie bei dieser heiligen Handlung durch eine andere Kaufmannsfrau vertreten, nämlich durch Johanna Margaretha von Brinck, geborene Conrad (1679–1745), eine Leipzigerin, die mit dem aus Braunschweig stammenden Handelsmann Balthasar Heinrich von Brinck (1667–1739) 1699 die Ehe einging. Gern wüsste man mehr zu den sich durch diese Patenschaft andeutenden Beziehungen der Familie Bach zu Kauf- und Handelsleuten, die ja in Leipzig traditionell eine große Bedeutung für die Stadt und ihre Entwicklung hatten. Doch da würden nur detailreiche soziologische Untersuchungen wirklich weiterhelfen.

An zweiter Stelle der Patenreihe steht auf dem Taufzettel Christian Wilhelm Ludewig (32–34) – das Taufbuch nennt ihn wie erwähnt an erster Stelle – (1675–1732). Er wird als „Königl. [Polnischer] und Churfürstl. Sachß. GleitsEinnahme bestalter Gleitsmann" vorgestellt, Angehöriger einer Berufsgruppe, deren Tätigkeit heute der Erklärung bedarf. Johann Christian Adelung (1732–1806), Verfasser wichtiger Sprachnachschlagewerke, erklärt dazu Folgendes: „eine obrigkeitliche Person, welche Reisende im Namen des Geleitsherrn geleitet, oder doch das Geleitsgeld von ihnen einnimmt".[20] Es handelt sich um das zeitgenössische Steuer-, Zoll- und Straßenwesen, das für Leipzig insbeson-

register moves her name to second position, perhaps because she was unable to attend in the baptism. She was represented by another merchant's wife, Johanna Margaretha von Brinck, née Conrad (1679–1745), a Leipzig resident who had married the trader Balthasar Heinrich von Brinck (1667–1739) of Braunschweig in 1699. One would like to know more about the Bach family's relations – expressed in the choice of these godparents – to merchants and tradesmen, who traditionally were of great influence on the city of Leipzig and its development. Only detailed sociological investigations might throw further light on the matter, however.

The second godparent mentioned on the baptismal slip was Christian Wilhelm Ludewig (1675–1732) – the baptismal register puts him in first position (lines 32–34). He is introduced as "Royal [Polish] and Electoral Saxon Escort Master", belonging to a professional group whose function today needs some explanation. Johann Christian Adelung (1732–1806), the author of important etymological dictionaries, explains that an "escort master" is "a person of authority who escorts merchant travelers in the name of the escort master or exacts escort taxes from them."[20] Customs and highway taxes were of great importance for Leipzig, especially because of the annual trade fairs. Escort bureaus were authorized to collect road taxes, which involved

43

dere wegen der jährlich stattfindenden Messen von sehr großer Bedeutung war. Geleitsämter hatten das obrigkeitliche Wegerecht auszuüben und den Wegezoll einzunehmen, was mit großen Finanzsummen verbunden war. Das Leipziger Geleitsamt hatte der Kurfürst zwischen 1687 und 1721 für anfänglich 23.000 Gulden sogar an die Stadt verpachtet. Neben anderen kurfürstlichen Behörden in Leipzig kam diesem im Bereich der Wirtschaft eine leitende Funktion zu. Ludewig, der aus Weißensee in Thüringen stammte, kam einst als Student nach Leipzig und unterstützte unter Bachs zweitem Amtsvorgänger, Thomaskantor Johann Schelle (1648–1701), den Chor als Altist.[21]
Der dritte Pate ist Gottlieb Christian Wagner (1664–1741), jüngster Sohn des ehemaligen und für Leipzig hochverdienten und frommen Bürgermeisters Paulus Wagner (1617–1697). Sein Beruf wird angegeben als „Handelsman, und E. E. Hochw. Raths GüterBestätiger". Letzteres bezeichnete damals die Tätigkeit eines Frachtmaklers oder offiziellen Spediteurs, zugleich verbunden mit Aufgaben der Steuerschätzung und der Akzise-Einnahmen auf bestimmte Waren. So war Gottlieb Christian Wagner als „Güterbestätiger" oder auch „Güterbestäter" dem Königlich Polnischen und Churfürstlich Sächsischen Ober-Accis-Amt zu Leipzig zugeordnet. Zusammen mit seinen beiden älteren Brüdern Gottfried Wagner (1652–1725) und Christian Wagner (1663–1693)

large amounts of money. The elector in fact had leased the escort rights to the city of Leipzig for the years between 1687 and 1721 for the initial amount of 23.000 thaler. Next to other electoral authorities in Leipzig escort masters exercised a pivotal economic function. Born in Weißensee, Thuringia, Ludewig came to Leipzig as a student and sang as an alto in the choir of Bach's second predecessor, the cantor of St. Thomas Johann Schelle (1648–1701).[21]
The third godfather was Gottlieb Christian Wagner (1664–1741), the youngest son of the highly respected and devout former mayor of Leipzig, Paulus Wagner (1617–1697). Wagner's profession was listed as "merchant and municipal artifier of goods." This described a freight broker or forwarding agent, who also assessed and collected the excise tax on certain goods. Gottlieb Christian Wagner was a "goods certifier" or "goods validator" assigned to the Royal Polish and Electoral Saxon chief collector at Leipzig as a "certifier of goods". Together with his two older brothers Gottfried Wagner (1652–1725) and Christian Wagner (1663–1693) he prepared the publication of an eight-volume hymnal, which attained great reputation as "Wagner's Hymnal" in Bach scholarship, not only because Bach owned a copy, but also because he used certain texts or text versions in his compositions.
The preface of the hymnal states that Gottlieb Christian Wagner, godfather

Andächtiger Seelen geistliches Brand- und Gantz-Opfer, Gesangbuch, Leipzig 1697

Spiritual Sacrifice of the Devouted Souls, Hymnal, Leipzig, 1697

bereitete er die Herausgabe jenes achtbändigen Gesangbuches vor, das als „Wagnersches Gesangbuch" u. a. in der Bachforschung großes Ansehen besitzt, weil nicht nur Bach es sein eigen nannte, sondern daraus auch bestimmte Texte bzw. Textversionen entnahm. Von Christian Gottlieb Bachs Namen gebendem Paten, Gottlieb Christian Wagner, ist in der Vorrede des Gesangbuchs zu erfahren, dass er „mit Versorgung des ziemlich kostbaren Verlages beschäftiget gewesen"[22] ist. Der Täufling wuchs of Christian Gottlieb Bach, "was occupied with the rather precious edition."[22] The infant did not live beyond early childhood, as is noted in an entry in the funeral ledger of Leipzig: "A young boy, 3 ½ years of age, Christian Gottlieb, son of Johann Sebastian Bach, cantor and musical director at St. Thomas School, died, ♂ [= Tuesday, September 21, 1728]."[23] It is possible that fear and sorrow over the child's early death led to a premature birth of the baby which Anna Magdalena was

nicht über das Kleinkindalter hinaus, wie aus dem Leichenbuch der Stadt Leipzig hervorgeht: „Ein Knäblein 3½ Jahr, Christian Gottlieb, Herrn Johann Sebastian Bachs, *Cantoris und Directoris Musices*, auf der Thomas Schule, st[arb]. ♂ [= Dienstag, dem 21. 9. 1728]."[23] Womöglich haben Schrecken und Kummer um diesen baldigen Tod des kleinen Jungen zur verfrühten Geburt des Kindes geführt, mit dem Anna Magdalena in dieser Zeit hochschwanger war; denn nur 2½ Wochen später wird 1728 Regina Johanna geboren werden (vgl. unten Taufzettel 5).

carrying at the time; for only two and a half weeks later Regina Johanna was born (see baptismal slip no. 5 below).

Taufzettel 3
Mit der Geburt des vierten Kindes und zweiten Tochter zweiter Ehe **Elisabeth Juliana Friederica** (1726–1781) Anfang April 1726 hatte die anwesende Familie eine Stärke von elf Mitgliedern erreicht. Wegen des immer wieder eintretenden Todes von Neugeborenen und Kleinkindern werden es in den Jahren bis 1750 trotz der Geburt weiterer Kinder nie wieder so viele Familienangehörige sein, die diese Wohnung miteinander teilen. Im Schulhaus am Thomaskirchhof lebten zu diesem Zeitpunkt vier Kinder erster Ehe – Catharina Dorothea (17), Wilhelm Friedemann (15), Carl Philipp Emanuel (11), Johann Gottfried Bernhard (knapp 10) – und vier Kinder zweiter Ehe: Christiana Sophia Henrietta (3), Gottfried Heinrich (2), Christian Gottlieb (1), das neugebore-

Baptismal Slip 3
With the birth of **Elisabeth Juliana Friederica** (1726–1781), the fourth child and second daughter of the second marriage, in early April, 1726, the Bach household had grown to include eleven persons. The frequent deaths of infants and young children, so universal at the time, meant that despite the birth of more children there were never again so many family members living together in the Thomasschule apartment. In the school building in Thomaskirchhof there were living at this time four children of Bach's first marriage – Catharina Dorothea (17), Wilhelm Friedemann (15), Carl Philipp Emanuel (11), Johann Gottfried Bernhard (nearly 10) – and four children of the second, Christiana Sophia Henrietta (3), Gottfried Heinrich (2), Christian Gottlieb (1), and the new-born infant girl as

ne Töchterchen sowie drei Erwachsene, Johann Sebastian mit Frau Anna Magdalena und Tante Friedelena Margaretha. Der Taufzettel hat wieder eine formularmäßige äußere Gestalt in einer schönen Kanzleischrift.	well as three adults: Johann Sebastian, his wife Anna Magdalena, and aunt Friedelena Margaretha. The baptismal slip again appears in official format in beautiful chancery handwriting.

[3]   *Zu St: Thomas 1726. den 5. Aprill.*

Vater ist Herr Johann Sebastian Bach, HochF. Anh. Cöth. Capellmeister, auch *Direct: Musices, und Cantor ad Schol: Thom: alhier.*

Mutter Frau Anna Magdalena, gebohrne Wilckin.

Kindes Nahme Elisabeth, Juliana, Friederica.

Pathen.
1.) *Frau Christiana Elisabeth, HErn Appellation-Rath D. Gottfried Wilhelm Küstners, des Raths alhier etc. EheLiebste.*

2.) *HE. Johann Friedrich Falckner, Jur: Utrq. Doctor, und Practicus alhier.*

3.) *Frau Juliana, HErn D. Carl Friedrich Romani, des Raths, und Stadt Richters alhier etc. EheLiebste.*

No $\frac{6}{138}$ ҁ. H M. R.

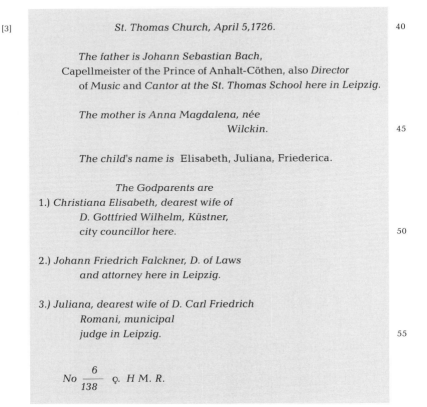

Daraus hebt sich bei aufmerksamem Betrachten der eigene Beitrag Johann Sebastian Bachs hervor; er ergänzt seine Berufsbezeichnung mit dem Titel des Anhalt-Köthenschen Kapellmeisters (41–42) und fügt ebenso eigenhändig den Namen des Kindes ein. Im Unterschied zur latinisierenden Namensaufschrift auf der Rückseite des Zettels schreibt Bach die deutsche

A closer look reveals the additions Johann Sebastian Bach made in his own hand: He supplements his professional title with that of capellmeister of the Prince of Anhalt-Cöthen (lines 41–42) and inserted the name of the new-born baby. Not using the Latinized name appearing on the reverse side of the slip, Bach entered the name in its German form. This agrees with the entry

Namensform. Das stimmt auch überein mit der Eintragung im Taufbuch.[24] Die Taufe vollzog am Freitag, den 5. April 1726, Subdiaconus M. Justus Gotthard Rabener, der an diesem Tage besonders gefordert war, da es sich um den 1. Bußtag des Jahres handelte, zu welchem er am Donnerstag schon die Vorbereitungsbetstunde und nun am Freitagnachmittag die Schlussbetstunde zu halten hatte. Wegen der drei weiteren Gottesdienste – Frühgottesdienst (7 Uhr, Thomaspastor Weise), Mittagspredigt (11.30 Uhr, Diaconus Sieber) und Vesperpredigt (13.30 Uhr, Archidiaconus Carpzov) – hat die Taufe wahrscheinlich im Anschluss an den Frühgottesdienst nach 10 Uhr stattgefunden.

Als Pate fungierte Johann Friedrich Falckner (1695–1755), Mitglied des Stadtrates, und auch die zwei Patinnen kamen aus den Kreisen der Stadtregierung: Christina – nicht Christiana wie der Taufzettel notiert – Elisabeth, geborene Winkler (1699–1768) heiratete als Siebzehnjährige den Ratsherrn Gottfried Wilhelm Küstner (1689–1762), der später Bürgermeister wurde. Nach Bachs Tod ist es Küstner, der sich entschieden gegen die Musik und für den Schuldienst des Nachfolgers ausspricht.[25] Die an dritter Stelle genannte Patin Juliana Romanus, geborene Jacob (1700–1747), ist die Ehefrau des Stadtrates Carl Friedrich Romanus (1679–1745), einem Verwandten des bedeutenden Leipziger Bürgermeisters Franz Conrad Romanus (1671–1745).

in the official baptism register.[24] The assistant deacon M. Justus Gotthard Rabener, performed the baptismal ceremony on Friday, April 5, 1726. On that day – it was the first day of Lent – he was particularly busy, having already conducted a preparatory prayer service on Thursday and still having to hold the final prayer service on Friday afternoon. As there were three additional services – an early service at 7 o'clock, conducted by the pastor at St. Thomas Weise, a noon service at 11:30 (Deacon Sieber) and a vesper service at 1:30 (Archdeacon Carpzov) – the baptism ceremony must have taken place after 10 o'clock, following the early service.

One of the godparents was Johann Friedrich Falckner (1695–1755), a member of the town council; and the two godmothers as well were connected with members of the municipal administration: Christina – not Christiana, as noted on the baptismal slip – Elisabeth, née Winkler (1699–1768) was married at the age of seventeen to the councillor Gottfried Wilhelm Küstner (1689–1762), who later became major. After Bach's death Küstner took a determined stand against his successor being a musician again rather than primarily a teacher.[25] The godmother Juliana Romanus, née Jacob (1700–1747), appears in third place. Juliana was the wife of the town councillor Carl Friedrich Romanus (1679–1745), a relative of the Leip-

»Ey, wie schmeckt der Coffee süße«, Kaffeekantate (BWV 211), Satz 4

"Ey! How sweet the coffee tastes!", Coffee Cantata (BWV 211), movement 4

Elisabeth Juliana Friederica ist die einzige Tochter, deren Hochzeit noch zu Lebzeiten des Vaters und der Mutter im Schulhaus in Leipzig gefeiert worden ist. Sie soll des Vaters Liebling gewesen sein. Den Kosenamen „Lieschen" verewigte der Vater in seiner berühmt gewordenen Kaffeekantate (BWV 211).

Die Hochzeit wurde durch das Aufgebot vorbereitet, das dreimal vollzogen wurde: in den Gottesdiensten des Sonntags nach Neujahr, 5. Januar 1749, des 1. Sonntags nach Epiphanias, 12. Januar 1749, und des 2. Sonntags nach Epiphanias, 19. Januar 1749. Zum ersten Termin verzeichnet das Traubuch der Thomaskirche zu Leipzig folgenden Eintrag:

Herr Johann Christoph *Altnicol*, *Organist* zu St. Wenzeslai in Naumburg. [und] Jungfer Elisabeth Juliana *Friderica*, Herrn Johann Sebastian Bachs, Königlich Pohlnischen und Churfürstlich Sächßischen Hoff-*Compositeurs*, Hochfürstlich-Sächßischen CapellMeisters, und *Cantoris* zu St. Thomas alhier eheliche älteste Jungfer Tochter, anderer Ehe.[26]

Für solche Meldungen gab es ebensolche Zettel zum Zweck der Abkündigung, wie sie uns in den Taufzetteln vorliegen. Ein ähnliches Aufgebot wurde auch in der Wenzelskirche zu Naumburg vorgetragen. Am Montag, dem 20. Januar 1749, fand vormittags um 10 Uhr der Traugottesdienst statt. Der knappe Eintrag im Traubuch zum

zig mayor, Franz Conrad Romanus (1671–1745).

Elisabeth Juliana Friederica was the only Bach daughter whose wedding was celebrated during her parents' lifetime in the St. Thomas School building. She was said to be her father's favorite. Her nickname "Lieschen" was immortalized by her father in his famous coffee cantata (BWV 211). The wedding was prepared by calling the banns three times – in the services of Sunday after New Year, January 5, 1749; of the 1st Sunday after Epiphany, January 12, 1749; and of the 2nd Sunday after Epiphany, January 19, 1749. The wedding registry of St. Thomas on the first of these dates has the following entry:

"Johann Christoph *Altnicol*, *organist* at St. *Wenceslas* in Naumburg [and] Elisabeth Juliana Friderica, oldest daughter from a second marriage of Johann Sebastian Bach, *composer* of the Royal Polish and Electoral Saxon court, capellmeister of the Duke of Saxony and *cantor* at St. Thomas."[26]

The slips used for these announcements were the same as those for baptisms. A similar announcement of the banns was made in the church of St. Wenceslas at Naumburg. The wedding took place on Monday, January 20, 1749, at 10 o'clock in the morning. The short entry in the marriage register recorded that the service was conducted by the archdeacon D. Christoph Wolle

51

Vollzug der Trauung vermerkt noch dazu, dass der Traugottesdienst von Archidiaconus D. Christoph Wolle (1700–1761) gehalten wurde, dem Beichtvater der Familie. Da es sich nur um eine sogenannte halbe Brautmesse handelte, wissen wir, dass es außer vierstimmigen Chorälen keine weitere Figuralmusik gab. Der Schwiegersohn Johann Christoph Altnickol (1719–1759) stammte aus der Oberlausitz, studierte seit März 1744 in Leipzig, gehörte zu Bachs späten Schülern in Leipzig und erhielt im Januar 1748 das Organistenamt in Niederwiesa bei Greiffenberg/Schlesien. Dieses verließ er aber bereits im September des gleichen Jahres für das besser dotierte an der Wenzelskirche zu Naumburg. Am 4. Oktober 1749 entband Elisabeth Juliana Friederica ihr erstes Kind, einen Jungen, der den Namen Johann Sebastian erhielt. Der Namen gebende Taufpate, sein Großvater Johann Sebastian Bach, konnte am 6. Oktober in Naumburg nicht anwesend sein und wurde vertreten. Doch das Kind verstarb bereits 14 Tage später wieder und wurde am 21. Oktober begraben. Aus der Ehe gingen noch zwei weitere Töchter hervor: Augusta Magdalena (1751–1809) wurde am 2. Juni 1751 in der Naumburger Wenzelskirche getauft. Unter den Paten befand sich ihre verwitwete Großmutter Anna Magdalena Bach aus Leipzig, die sich aber vertreten ließ. Augusta Magdalena war seit 1777 mit dem Siegellack-

(1700–1761), confessor of the family. As this was not a solemn service but rather a so-called "halbe Brautmesse", there was no figured music other than four-part chorales. The son-in-law, Johann Christoph Altnickol (1719–1759), who hailed from Upper Lusatia and had been a student at Leipzig since March 1744, was one of Bach's last pupils. In January 1748 he assumed the position of organist in Niederwiesa near Greiffenberg/ Silesia. In September of that year he left, however, for the better-paying position in Naumburg. On October 4, 1749, Elisabeth Juliana Friederica gave birth to her first child, a boy who was named Johann Sebastian. The godparent, his grandfather Johann Sebastian Bach, could not be present in Naumburg on October 6 and was represented by someone else. The baby died 14 days later and was buried on October 21. Later two daughters were born of this marriage. Augusta Magdalena (1751–1809) was baptized in the Naumburg Wenzelskirche on June 2, 1751. Listed as godparent was her widowed grandmother Anna Magdalena Bach who, however, was not present at the baptismal service. Augusta Magdalena was married in 1777 in Leipzig to the sealing wax manufacturer Ernst Friedrich Ahlefeld (1752–1787). The second daughter, Juliana Wilhelmina (1754–1818), was also born in Naumburg, on July 30, 1754 and married the Leipzig printing apprentice Heinrich

fabrikanten Ernst Friedrich Ahlefeld (1752–1787) in Leipzig verheiratet. Die zweite Tochter Juliana Wilhelmina (1754–1818), geboren am 30. Juli 1754 ebenfalls in Naumburg, wird 1792 den in Leipzig lebenden Buchdruckergesellen Heinrich Friedrich Anton Prüfer heiraten (um 1756–1815). Elisabeth Juliana Friedericas Ehemann Johann Christoph Altnickol starb verhältnismäßig jung bereits Ende Juli 1759 in Naumburg, woraufhin seine Witwe 1760 wieder nach Leipzig zurückzog. Offenbar hatte sie ihren behinderten Bruder Gottfried Heinrich (vgl. Taufzettel 1) bis zu dessen Tod 1763 in anderweitiger Obhut in Naumburg lassen können, denn eine Leipziger Kuratorenakte von 1765 redet davon, dass sich die „Altnickolin seit 5. Jahren allhier wohnhaft befindet".[27] Sie teilte mit ihren beiden Töchtern und den drei unverheirateten Schwestern eine Wohnung am Neukirchhof und wurde unter der Berufsbezeichnung einer Näherin als Mieterin geführt. Am 24. August 1781 starb sie nur knapp zwei Wochen nach ihrer jüngeren Schwester Johanna Carolina (vgl. Taufzettel 11). Offensichtlich grassierte damals in Leipzig eine ansteckende Krankheit, die als „rote Ruhr" bezeichnet wurde. Die allein verbliebene jüngste Schwester Regina Susanna (vgl. Taufzettel 12) wird zu diesem Zeitpunkt die Wohnung am Neukirchhof aufgegeben haben und in eine kleinere der Quergasse gezogen sein.

Friedrich Anton Prüfer (ca. 1756–1815) in 1792. The husband of Elisabeth Juliana Friederica, Johann Christoph Altnickol, died in Naumburg toward the end of July, 1759 at a relatively young age, whereupon his widow returned to Leipzig the following year. She had apparently been able to leave her disabled brother Gottfried Heinrich (see baptismal slip no. 1) in good care in Naumburg, where he died in 1763, since a Leipzig guardian document noted in 1765: "The Altnickolin has been in residence in our town for five years."[27] She shared a flat at the Neukirchhof with her two daughters and her three unmarried sisters and was recorded as a tenant with the occupational title of a needlewoman. She died on August 24, 1781, two weeks after her younger sister Johanna Carolina (cf. baptismal slip no. 11). A contagious disease, described as "red dysentery", was raging in Leipzig at that time. The youngest sister Regina Susanna (baptismal slip no. 12) then was the only one left; she probably gave up the apartment at the Neukirchhof at that time to move into smaller quarters in the Quergasse.

Taufzettel 4

Nur 14 Tage nach den aufregenden Wochen um Komposition und Aufführung der Trauerode (BWV 198) für die verstorbene sächsische Kurfürstin Christiane Eberhardine (1671–1727) wurde Anna Magdalena am 30. Oktober 1727 von einem Knaben entbunden: **Ernestus Andreas**. Das Kind wurde an seinem Geburtstag sogleich getauft. Dies zeigt, dass Gefahr im Verzuge war: Der Knabe verstarb bereits nach zwei Tagen wieder, wie das Leichenbuch vermerkt.[28]

Baptismal Slip 4

Only 14 days after the exciting weeks of composing and performing the mourning ode (BWV 198) for Christiane Eberhardine, the deceased Saxon Electress (1671–1727), on October 30, 1727 Anna Magdalena gave birth to a baby boy: **Ernestus Andreas**. The infant was baptized the same day. This indicates that there must have been serious concerns about the baby's health, and indeed, according to the death registry he died after only two days.[28]

[4]   *Tauff-Zettel zu St: Thomas den 30 8br: 1727*

Des Kindes Vater ist Herr Johann Sebastian Bach Hochfürstl. Anhalt Köthenischer Capell=Meister und Cantor zu St: Thomas alhier.

Die Mutter Frau Anna Magdalena gebohrne Wilckin
Des Kindes Nahme
Ernestus, Andreas,

Die Pathen sind
1. *Herr D. Johann Ernst Kregel, Königl. Pohl. und Churfl. Sächß. Hoff= und Justitien Rath.*
2. *Frau* Magdalena Sibylla, *Tit Herrn* ~~Leonhardt~~ Gottfried Leonhard *Baudisii J. U. D. und StadtRichters alhier* ~~hinterl.~~ Frau ~~Wittbe~~ Eheliebste.
3. *Herr Andreas Rivinus J. U. D. alhier.*

No $\frac{41}{397.}$ ⚷ *H. D. C.*

60
65
70
75

[4] Baptismal slip, St. Thomas, October 30, 1727

> The child's father is Johann Sebastian
> Bach, Capellmeister of the Prince of Anhalt Köthen
> and cantor here at St. Thomas.
>
> The mother is Anna Magdalena, née
> Wilckin
> The childs name
> Ernestus, Andreas,
>
> The godparents are
> 1. D. Johann Ernst Kregel, Royal Polish and
> Electoral Saxon legal councillor
> 2. Magdalena Sibylla, dearest wife ~~widow~~ of ~~Leonhardt~~ Gottfried
> Leonhard Baudisius, doctor of laws and municipal judge here
> in Leipzig.
> 3. Andreas Rivinus, doctor of laws.
>
> No $\frac{41}{397}$ ~~4~~ H. D. C.

Die Taufe, als 41. im Monat Oktober und als 397. im Jahr 1727 registriert, vollzog an jenem Donnerstag nach dem 20. Sonntag nach Trinitatis Archidiconus D. Johann Gottlob Carpzov (1679–1767). Als Paten waren gebeten und erschienen der Ratsherr Johann Ernst Kregel (1686–1737), ein Jurist an dem in Leipzig stationierten Oberhofgericht, die Ehefrau des Stadtrichters Gottfried Leonhard Baudisius (1683–1739), Magdalena Sibylla Baudisius, geborene Winkler (1695–1752) und der

The baptism on the Thursday following the 20th Sunday after Trinity was performed by Archdeacon D. Johann Gottlob Carpzov (1679–1767); this was the 41st baptism in October and the 397th in 1727. The godparents were the councillor Johann Ernst Kregel (1686–1737), a lawyer at the supreme court in Leipzig, Magdalena Sibylla Baudisius, née Winkler (1695–1752), the wife of the town judge Gottfried Leonhard Baudisius (1683–1739), and the lawyer D. Andreas Florens Rivinus (1701–1761).

Johann Gottlob Carpzov
(1679–1767), Pfarrer der
Thomaskirche

Johann Gottlob Carpzov
(1679–1767), pastor
at St. Thomas

Jurist D. Andreas Florens Rivinus (1701–1761). Bach selbst trägt auf diesem Taufzettel nicht nur den Namen des Kindes (66) ein, sondern auch den Namen und den Stand der an zweiter Stelle genannten Patin und verändert den Namen ihres Ehemannes (70–72) und deshalb auch ihren Stand, weil der Schreiber des Taufzettels zunächst mit dem Vater des Ehemanns gerechnet hatte, der ebenfalls Stadtrichter gewesen war. Die Bestimmung des jüngeren Juristen Rivinus zum Paten ist nach dem Paten Graff für Gottfried Heinrich (Taufzettel 1) ein weiteres Merkmal der Beziehung zu Mitgliedern der Familie Rivinus, die auch noch später weitere Belege erhält (vgl. Taufzettel 10).

Bach recorded not only the name of the baby (line 66) on the baptismal slip, but also the name and social status of the godmother mentioned in second position. He changed the name of her husband (lines 70–72), and therefore her family status, because initially the writer of the baptismal slip had assumed that the husband's father, who also had been town judge, would be the godparent. The appointment of the young lawyer Rivinus as godparent was, after Graff had been chosen as godparent for Gottfried Heinrich (baptismal slip no. 1), another indication of the close relationship of the Bach and Rivinus families, for which we find further proof in later years (cf. baptismal slip no. 10).

Johann Ernst Kregel (1686–1737), Jurist

Johann Ernst Kregel (1686–1737), Jurist

Taufzettel 5

Mit dem Taufzettel des sechsten Kindes zweiter Ehe, der Tochter **Regina Johanna** (1728–1733), halten wir ein in mehrfacher Hinsicht besonders kostbares und zugleich interessantes Dokument in der Hand. Es ist – abgesehen von der näheren familiären Zuordnung der Ernesti-Töchter (95–98, linker Rand) und den Registrierangaben einschließlich des Datums und des Pfarrernamens (99–101) – vollständig von Bachs eigener Hand geschrieben. Es handelte sich um eine „Nothtauffe" (101), es erlaubt einen interessanten Blick in das Haus der Bachschen Familie am Thomaskirchhof im Oktober 1728:

Baptismal Slip 5

The baptismal slip for the sixth child of the second marriage, the daughter **Regina Johanna** (1728–1733), is a particularly valuable and interesting document. It was filled out by Bach himself, except for the family details of the Ernesti daughters (lines 95–98, left margin) and such registration details as the date and the pastor's name (lines 99–101). This was an emergency baptism (line 101), which provides an interesting glimpse at the Bach family in October, 1728:

[5] Regina Johanna Bachin,

    Die Tauffzeügen, so abwesend, heißen,

(1) Frau Anna Catharina Meißnerin, gebohrene Wülckin,
Herrn Georg, Christian, Meißners, Hochf. Sächs.
Weißenfelsischen HoffFourierers Ehe Liebste.
(2) Frau Johanna Christina Krebsin, geb. Wülckin,
Herrn Johann Andreas Krebsens, Hochf.
Anhalt. Zerbistischen Hoff und Feld Trompeters
auch Camer u. Hoff Musici EheLiebste.
(3) Herr Johann Caspar Wülcke, Hochf. Anh.
Zerbstischer Hoff u. FeldTrompeter, auch
Camer u. HoffMusicus.

    Die Eltern heißen
Johann Sebastian Bach, Hochf. Anh. Cöthenischer
Capellmeister, wie auch Director Chori
    Musici Lipsiensis u. Cantor zu S. Thomae.
Anna Magdalena, gebohrne Wülckin. etc.

    Die Vice Pathen waren

H. M. Joh. Heinrich (1) Die Junfer Regina Christina Ernestin, und
Ernestis. zu St. Th: (2) Deren Jungfer Schwester Johanna Benedicta Ernestin, dañ
Rect: u. Prof: Publ: (3) Herr Georg, Heinrich, Ludewig, Schwanenberger,
Poes: Jfr. Töchter   HochF. Braunschw. Camer Musicus.

$$No \ \frac{11}{327} \quad \odot \quad \begin{array}{l} d.\ 10.\ 8br: \\ H.\ M.\ R \end{array} \quad \text{(Nothtauffe.}$$

[5] Regina Johanna Bachin,

The godparents, in absentia, are,

(1) Anna Catharina Meißnerin, née Wülckin,
dearest wife of Georg, Christian, Meißner,
purveyor to the Princely Court of Saxe-Weißenfels.
(2) Johanna Christina Krebs, née Wülckin,
dearest wife of Johann Andreas Krebs,
court and field trumpeter as well as chamber
and court musician at the Court of Anhalt-Zerbst.
(3) Johann Caspar Wülcke, court and
field trumpeter as well as chamber
and court musician at the Court of Anhalt-Zerbst.

The parents are
Johann Sebastian Bach, Capellmeister of the Prince
of Anhalt-Cöthen as well as Director of Music
in Leipzig and Cantor at St. Thomas.
Anna Magdalena, née Wülckin. etc.

The representative Godparents were

daughters of   (1) Regina Christina Ernesti, and
Johann Heinrich Ernesti, (2) her sister Johanna Benedicta Ernesti, and
rector of St. Thomas   (3) Georg, Heinrich, Ludewig, Schwanenberger,
and professor of rhetoric.   chamber musician at the court in Brunswick.

No $\dfrac{11}{327}$ ☉   *d. 10. 8br:*
                  H. M. R
                               (emergency baptism.

Die eingangs angestellten Überlegungen zum Reglement und was zu beachten war, bei der Anmeldung einer Taufe, sind im Falle einer Nottaufe außer Kraft gesetzt. Die Situation der Lebensgefahr des neugeborenen Kindes machte es erforderlich, dass sofort gehandelt wurde. Entweder war es die Hebamme selbst, die die Nottaufe vollzog, oder es wurde ein naher Angehöriger tätig. Im Taufbuch der Thomaskirche ist abschließend ausdrücklich der Grund der Nottaufe festgestellt: „Aus Schwachheit zu Hause getaufft."[29] Die fast durchgängig autografe Gestalt des Taufzettels lässt sogar den Schluss zu, Bach selbst sei die wesentlich handelnde Person gewesen und habe sein Töchterchen getauft. Das gültige Regelwerk für alle Gottesdienste und Kasualien, die Agende, handelt ausdrücklich „Von der Noth-Tauffe".[30] Diese war von der Wittenberger Reformation einst infolge anerkennenswerter mittelalterlicher Kirchengebräuche beibehalten worden. Man solle – so wird allerdings ausdrücklich mahnend hervorgehoben –

> nicht leichtlich zu der Noth-Tauffe eilen ..., wenn es aber die hohe Nothdurfft erfordert, daß man tauffen soll und muß, daß die, so dabey sind, unsern HErrn GOTT zuvor anruffen, und ein Vater Unser beten: Wenn solches geschehen, alsdann darauf tauffen im Namen des Vaters, und des Sohnes, und des Heiligen Geistes. Und daß man dann nicht zweyffelt,

In the case of an emergency baptism the customary rules and practices were suspended. The life-threatening situation of the new-born infant called for immediate action. Either it was the midwife herself who performed the emergency baptism, or a close relative. The reason for the emergency baptism, is explicitly noted in the baptismal register of St. Thomas Church: "Due to her weakness she was baptized at home."[29] As nearly all of the baptismal slips were written by J. S. Bach himself, this may suggest that he took the initiative and baptized his infant daughter. The regulations for worship and any other liturgical situation that might arise, the "Agende", includes a section on "emergency baptism."[30] This traditional medieval practice had been retained by the Wittenberg Reformation as a commendable church custom.

> "As cannot be urged too emphatically, one must not resort lightheartedly to emergency baptism... If, however, an emergency situation mandates that one shall and must baptize, then those present shall offer a supplication to our God and pray the Lord's Prayer. When this has taken place the child should be baptized in the name of the Father and the Son and the Holy Spirit. When this is done, there is no reasen to doubt that the baby has been properly and sufficiently baptized and should not be baptized again in the church or in

das Kind sey recht und gnugsam getaufft, und nicht soll anderweit in der Kirchen oder sonst getaufft werden. Doch soll man solch Kind, wenn es am Leben bleibt, in die Kirche tragen, daß der Pfarrherr die Leute frage, ob sie auch gewiß seyn, daß das Kind recht getaufft sey, und mit was Weise und Worten sie es getaufft haben?
Der Vermerk der Registriernummer (99–101) – die 11. Taufe im Monat Oktober und die 327. Taufe im Jahr 1728 – sowie Taufdatum und Name des Taufpfarrers, M. Rabener (vgl. Taufzettel 1) werden der zuletzt gemachten Anweisung gerecht; Diaconus Rabener hat in dem angegebenen Sinne als diensthabender Pfarrer gehandelt. Auf dem Taufzettel sind von Bach – der Erinnerung nach angeordnet – alle wesentlichen Angaben gemacht; ein Vergleich mit den anderen von den Leichenschreibern vorbereiteten formularhaften Zetteln zeigt aber, dass Bach die Reihenfolge umkehrt: Zuerst nennt er den Namen des Kindes, dann die Paten und zuletzt die Eltern. Anschließend fügt er die stellvertretenden Paten hinzu und vermerkt am Schluss die Nottaufe.
Aus der Wahl der Paten geht hervor, dass man sich einig geworden war, die bisher unberücksichtigten familiären Beziehungen zu bevorzugen: Die erste Patin Anna Catharina Meißner (1688–1757) ist die älteste Schwester Anna Magdalenas, seit 1710 verheiratet mit dem Weißenfelser Hoftrompeter

another way. But the infant is to be taken to the church (if the baby is still alive) where the pastor will ask the family whether they are certain that the child was properly baptized and how and with what words this was done?"
The entry of the registration number (lines 99–101) – the 11th baptism in October and the 327th baptism in the year 1728 – as well as the date of baptism and the name of the baptizing pastor, M. Rabener (cf. baptismal slip no. 1), confirm the instructions quoted above; Deacon Rabener had acted in the appropriate manner as the parish pastor on duty. On the baptismal slip Bach entered all the essential information from memory; a comparison with the other documents prepared by the registrar of deaths shows, however, that Bach inverted the usual order: First the mentioned the name of the child, then the godparents and finally the parents. Then he added the representative godparents and at the end noted the fact that this was an emergency baptism.
The choice of godparents suggests that the family now had decided to ask relatives, who had been ignored until then. The first godparent, Anna Catharina Meißner (1688–1757), was Anna Magdalena's oldest sister, married since 1710 to the Weißenfels court trumpeter Georg Christian Meißner († 1730). The second godparent was her younger sister Johan-

Georg Christian Meißner († 1730). Bei der zweiten handelt es sich um deren jüngere Schwester Johanna Christina Krebs (1695–1753), seit 1716 verheiratet mit dem Weißenfelser und späteren Zerbster Hoftrompeters Johann Andreas Krebs († 1748). Als dritter Pate ist Anna Magdalenas Bruder Johann Caspar Wilcke d.J. (1691–1766) angeben. Weder aus Weißenfels noch aus Zerbst konnte man so rasch in Leipzig sein, um das Patenamt bei einem in Lebensgefahr schwebenden Kind auszuüben. Denn Anna Magdalena war womöglich von der Geburt überrascht worden, und es liegt der Schluss nahe, dass Schrecken und Kummer um den frühen Tod des kleinen Christian Gottlieb (vgl. Taufzettel 2), der knapp drei Wochen zuvor mit 3 ½ Jahren verstorben war, eventuell sogar eine Frühgeburt ausgelöst haben.
Die Wahl der stellvertretenden Paten erlaubt eine Momentaufnahme der häuslichen Situation im Oktober 1728: Die Familie besteht zu dieser Zeit nicht nur aus den vier Kindern erster Ehe, drei Kindern zweiter Ehe, den Eltern einschließlich der Tante Friedelena Margaretha, sondern hatte auch für längere Zeit jenen Hochfürstlich-Braunschweigischen Kammermusikus Georg Heinrich Ludwig Schwanberger aufgenommen (1696–1774), der vom Spätherbst 1727 an in Leipzig weilte. Wie lange er noch blieb, ist schwer zu sagen; erst 1731 taucht er in Wolfenbüttel wieder auf.[31] Er war ebenso na Christina (1695–1753), who in 1716 had married Johann Andreas Krebs († 1748), a court trumpeter at Weißenfels and later at Zerbst. The third godparent was Anna Magdalena's brother Johann Caspar Wilcke the younger (1691–1766). It was not possible to get from either Weißenfels or Zerbst to Leipzig quickly enough to carry out the godparental responsibilities for an infant whose life was in danger. Anna Magdalena may have been surprised by an early delivery; perhaps her fear and sorrow about the early death of her little son Christian Gottlieb, (baptismal slip no. 2), who had died at the age of 3 ½ years some three weeks earlier, triggered a premature birth. The choice of the representative godparents allows a glimpse at the domestic situation in the Bach household in October 1728: At that time the family consisted not only of the four children of Bach's first marriage, the three children of the second marriage, the parents and aunt Friedelena Margaretha, but living also with the family for some time was Georg Heinrich Ludwig Schwanberger (1696–1774), chamber musician at the court of Brunswick, who arrived in Leipzig in the late fall of 1727. The sources do not tell us how long he stayed, but by 1731 he was residing in Wolfenbüttel again.[31] He was as easily persuaded to be a representative godfather as were the two daughters of the elderly rector of the St. Thomas

unkompliziert für die Übernahme eines stellvertretenden Patenamtes zu gewinnen wie die beiden Töchter des greisen Thomasschulrektors Ernesti, Regina Christiana (1702–1729) und Johanna Benedicta (1705–1776), die man gleichsam nur „von nebenan" zu rufen brauchte. Die jüngere von beiden Schwestern wird sich ein reichliches Jahr später mit dem Rechtskonsulenten Moerlin verheiraten, der dann beim nächsten Kind der Familie Bach in den Kreis der Bachschen Paten tritt (vgl. Taufzettel 6).

Regina Johanna gehörte zu den Kindern des Ehepaares Bach, die über das Kindesalter nicht hinaus gelangen; sie starb im Alter von 4 ½ Jahren am 25. April 1733.

School, Ernesti: Regina Christiana (1702–1729) and Johanna Benedicta (1705–1776), who only needed to be called from next door. A year later the younger of the two sisters married the legal councillor Moerlin, who joined the circle of the godparents of the Bach family when the next child was born (see baptismal slip 6). Regina Johanna was one of the children of Johann Sebastian and Anna Magdalena who did not survive to adulthood; on April 25, 1733 she died at the age of 4 ½ years.

Taufzettel 6

In der Mitte des Jahres 1729 starb die ältere Schwester von Bachs erster Frau Maria Barbara, Friedelena Margaretha (1675–1729), im Alter von knapp 54 Jahren. Sie war unverheiratet geblieben und seit den Weimarer Zeiten der damals jungen Familie als Hilfe dem Haushalt beigetreten. Es war der Tag, an dem Johann Sebastian Bach 21 Jahre später ebenfalls sterben würde, der 28. Juli.
Anna Magdalena befand sich zu dieser Zeit bereits im vierten Monat einer erneuten Schwangerschaft. Die Tochter **Christiana Benedicta Louisa** kam wahrscheinlich am letzten Tag des Jahres, am 31. Dezember 1729

Baptismal Slip 6

In mid-1729 Friedelena Margaretha (1675–1729), the older sister of Johann Sebastian Bach's first wife Maria Barbara, died at the age of nearly 54 years. She never married and had joined the Bach household to help out the young family in Weimar. She died on July 28, the exact day on which, 21 years later, Johann Sebastian Bach would also die.
At that time Anna Magdalena was in the fourth month of a new pregnancy. Her daughter **Christiana Benedicta Louisa** was probably born on the last day of the year, December 31, 1729. She was the seventh child and fourth daughter of the second marriage.

zur Welt. Sie war das siebente Kind und vierte Tochter zweiter Ehe; so sind mit der Neugeborenen nun vier kleine Kinder zweiter Ehe am Leben: Gottfried Heinrich (knapp 6 Jahre), Elisabeth Juliana Friederica (3 ½ Jahre), Regina Johanna (reichlich 1 Jahr). Am Neujahrstag, Sonntag, dem 1. Januar 1730 – der Oberleichenschreiber irrt einen Augenblick bei der Niederschrift der neuen Jahreszahl –, empfing das kleine Mädchen in der Thomaskirche die heilige Taufe. Doch nur vier Tage später verstarb das Kind wieder und wurde am Donnerstag, dem 5. Januar beerdigt.[32]
Anders als auf dem formal wieder wie üblich aufgebauten und gestalteten Taufzettel fehlen im Taufbuch der dritte Vorname des Kindes, „Louisa" (119), und der zweite Vorname der ersten Patin „Sophia" (110). Bachs Dienstbezeichnung variiert: Während der Taufzettel allgemeiner formuliert, „Director Musices und Cantor zu St: Thomae alhier" (105–106), ist das Taufbuch in seiner Angabe spezifischer und damit exakter, „Director Musices u. Cantor an der Schulen zu St. Thom. alhier". Alle anderen Angaben stimmen überein.

Apart from the new-born infant, three young children of the second marriage were still alive: Gottfried Heinrich (almost 6 years of age), Elisabeth Juliana Friederica (3 ½ years) and Regina Johanna (just over one year). On New Year's Day of 1730, a Sunday – the senior registrar of deaths at first made a mistake when writing down the numerals of the new year – the baby girl received holy baptism in St. Thomas. But she died only four days later and was buried on Thursday, January 5.[32] Unlike the customary format of the baptismal slips, the baptismal register does not record her third Christian name, "Louisa" (line 119), nor the second Christian name of the first godparent, "Sophia" (line 110). Bach's titles were stated in several ways. While the baptismal slip spoke generally of "music director and cantor here at St. Thomas" (line 105–106), the baptismal register was more specific and thus more exact, recording "musical director and cantor at the school here at St. Thomas." All other details match.

[6]

Leipzig den 1 Januarii
1730

Des Kindes Vater ist H. Johann Sebastian
Bach Director Musices und Cantor zu St: 105
Thomae alhier

Die Mutter Frau Anna Magdalena gebohrne Wilckin

Die Pathen sind
1. *Jungfer Sophia Benedicta, H. D. Johann Gottlob Carpzovs P. P. u. ArchiDiaconi zu St: Thomae älteste Jfr. Tochter.*

2. *HE. D. Christian Gottfried Moerlin. Rechts Consulent alhier*

3. *Frau Catharina Louisa, H. Johann Gottlieb Gleditschens, Buch Händlers alhier Frau Eheliebste.*

Des Kindes Nahme.
Christiana Benedicta Louisa.

No $\dfrac{3}{3}$ ⊙ H. D. C.

110

115

120

[6]

Leipzig, January 1, 1730

The child's father is Johann Sebastian Bach, Director of Music and Cantor here at St. Thomae
The mother is Anna Magdalena, née Wilckin

The godparents are
1. Sophia Benedicta, oldest daughter of D. Johann Gottlob Carpzov, archdeacon at St. Thomas.

2. D. Christian Gottfried Moerlin. attorney.

105

110

65

3. *Catharina Louisa, wife of the bookseller*
   Johann Gottlieb Gleditsch
   here in Leipzig

   The child's name is
   Christiana Benedicta Louisa.

No $\dfrac{3}{3}$ ☉ H. D. C.

Bei der Wahl der Paten werden zwei Tendenzen fortgesetzt, die schon früher zu beobachten waren: Die Tochter des Archidiaconus von St. Thomas (110–112), Sophia Benedicta Carpzov (1711–1774), repräsentiert die verzweigte Carpzovische Familie, der wir bereits in Regina Maria Ernesti, geborene Carpzov, unter den Paten von Gottfried Heinrich (Taufzettel 1) begegneten. Ihr Vater ist zugleich der Taufpfarrer (121): Johann Gottlob Carpzov (1679–1767), zu dieser Zeit noch an der Thomaskirche und als Extraordinarius an der Theologischen Fakultät tätig; gegen Ende des eben begonnenen Jahres wird er nach Lübeck als Superintendent gehen. An zweiter Stelle fungiert als Pate der Rechtskonsulent D. Christian Gottfried Moerlin (1703–1754); er war schon bei Regina Johanna Bach (Taufzettel 5) als künftiger Ehemann der stellvertretenden Patin Johanna Benedicta Ernesti (1705–1776) genannt worden (113–114). Die

We have already had occasion to note the continuation of two trends in the choice of godparents: The daughter of the archdeacon of St. Thomas (lines 110–112), Sophia Benedicta Carpzov (1711–1774), represented the extensive Carpzov family, which we encountered already in the person of Regina Maria Ernesti, née Carpzov, as one of the godparents of Gottfried Heinrich (baptismal slip no. 1). Her father was also the pastor who officiated at the baptism (line 121): Johann Gottlob Carpzov (1679–1767), who was at that time both at St. Thomas and professor of the theological faculty; at the end of that year he became superintendent in Lübeck. The second godparent was the legal councillor D. Christian Gottfried Moerlin (1703–1754); on the baptismal slip of Regina Johanna Bach (no. 5) he was mentioned (lines 113–114) as the future husband of the godparent Johanna Benedicta Ernesti (1705–1776). The third godparent was

dritte Patenstelle schließlich erhält die Ehefrau des in Leipzig wirkenden bedeutenden Buchhändlers und Verlegers Johann Gottlieb Gleditsch (1688–1738) Catharina Louisa, geborene Lange (1700–1779) (115–117). Beachtenswert ist dabei der Zeitpunkt dieser Patenwahl; denn gerade in diesen Wochen entspann sich jener Konflikt unter den Leipziger Buchdruckern und Verlegern, den man als „Verlegerkrieg"[33] bezeichnet: Auf der einen Seite stand der junge Johann Heinrich Zedler (1706–1751) zusammen mit Johann Christoph Gottsched (1700–1766) und einer Reihe ihm verpflichteter Gelehrter für das geplante „Universal-Lexicon"; auf der anderen Seite standen Buchhändler mit alteingesessenen Verlagshäusern Thomas Fritsch (1666–1726; Verlagshaus bis 1741), Johann Ludwig Gleditsch (1663–1741), Johann Gottlieb Gleditsch (1688–1738) und Johann Friedrich Gleditsch d.J. († 1744), die je Speziallexika in ihrem Verlag anboten und nun befürchteten, Zedler werde für sein Lexikon ihre Editionen ausbeuten.

Taufzettel 7
Wenige Tage vor der ersten Aufführung der Markuspassion (BWV 247) am 23. März und wenige Wochen vor dem Umzug der Familie in ein Ausweichquartier, der wegen des Umbaus und der Sanierung der Thomasschule nötig wurde, brachte Anna Magdalena wohl am 17. März 1731 **Christiana Dorothea**, achtes Kind, fünfte Tochter

Catharina Louisa Gleditsch, née Lange (1700–1779) (lines 115–117), wife of the influential Leipzig bookseller and publisher, Johann Gottlieb Gleditsch (1688–1738). The timing of the choice of these godparents was remarkable as a conflict known as the "publishers' war" of Leipzig printers and publishing houses developed during those weeks.[33] On one side was the youthful Johann Heinrich Zedler (1706–1751), together with Johann Christoph Gottsched (1700–1766) and several scholars who had agreed to participate in a proposed "universal encyclopedia." On the opposite side were the booksellers of the old and established publishing houses, such as Thomas Fritsch (1666–1726, publishing house until 1741), Johann Ludwig Gleditsch (1663–1741), Johann Gottlieb Gleditsch (1688–1738) and Johann Friedrich Gleditsch the younger († 1744), who published specialized dictionaries and feared that Zedler would exploit their publications for his encyclopedia.

Baptismal slip 7
A few days before the first performance of the Passion of St. Mark (BWV 247) on March 23 and a few weeks before the family's move to temporary accommodations – made necessary because of the renovation and expansion of the St. Thomas School building, the home also of the Bach family – Anna Magdalena gave birth to a baby girl, **Christiana Dorothea**, born probably

zweiter Ehe zur Welt. Aber auch dieses Kind hatte kein langes Leben; bereits am 31. August des Folgejahres verstarb das 1½-jährige Mädchen.³⁴ Die Taufe – es ist die 30. im Monat März und die 103. im laufenden Jahr – vollzieht wieder Subdiaconus Rabener. Bachs Beitrag zu dem Taufschein besteht wie gewohnt in der eigenhändigen Hinzufügung des Namens (141).

on March 17, 1731. Christiana was the eighth child and fifth daughter of Bach's second marriage. She did not live long, dying on August 31 of the following year at the age of 1½ years.³⁴ The baptism – the 30th in the month of March and the 103rd of the year – was again performed by the assistant deacon Rabener. Bach's contribution to the baptismal slip consisted, as was customary, of inserting the

[7]

        Leipzig
     den 18 Martii
       1731   125
Des Kindes Vater ist
Herr Johann Sebastian Bach, Direct:
Musices und Cantor zu St: Thomae
      Die Mutter
Frau Anna Magdalena geb. Wilckin   130

     Die Pathen sind
1. Jfr. Christiana Sibylla, H. George Hein=
   rich Bosens Kauff= und Handelsmanns
   alhier älteste Jfr. Tochter.
2. H. M. Andreas Winckler,   135
3, Fr. Christiana Dorothea, H. M. Johann
   Christian Hebenstreits, ConRectoris zu
   St: Thomae und Ling: Sanct: Professoris
   Publ: Ord: alhier Frau Eheliebste.

      Des Kindes Nahme.   140
       Christiana Dorothea.

No $\dfrac{30}{103}$ ☉ H. M. R.

[7]
Leipzig
March 18,
1731
The child's father is
Johann Sebastian Bach, director
of Music and Cantor at St. Thomas
The mother is
Anna Magdalena, née Wilckin.

The godparents are
1. *Christiana Sibylla, oldest daughter*
   of George Heinrich Bose,
   merchant in Leipzig.
2. *M. Andreas Winckler.*
3, *Christiana Dorothea, dearest wife*
   of M. Johann Christian
   Hebenstreit, Conrector at St. Thomas
   and Professor of Sacred Scripture.

The child's name is
Christiana Dorothea.

No $\dfrac{30}{103}$ ⊙ H. M. R.

Unter den Paten taucht mit Christiana Sibylla Bose (1711–1749) zum ersten Mal eine Vertreterin der Kaufmannsfamilie vom Hause gegenüber auf (132–134).
Da ihr Patenkind so früh wieder verstorben war, bat man Christiana Sibylla Bose 1735 erneut zur Patin (Taufzettel 10). Ihr, der reichlich zehn Jahre Jüngeren, schenkte – inzwischen

baby's name in his own hand (line 141). With Christiana Sibylla Bose (1711–1749) for the first time a member of the merchant family living in the house opposite the Bach residence appeared as godparent (lines 132–134). Since her godchild had died so young, Christiana Sibylla Bose was asked again to be godparent in 1735 (baptismal slip no. 10). In 1741 Anna Magdalena presented Christiana,

69

Johann Jacob Rambach, Betrachtungen über das gantze Leiden Christi, Jena 1732; Widmung Anna Magdalenas für Christiana Sibylla Bose

Johann Jacob Rambach, Contemplations about the Whole Suffering of Christ, Jena 1732; Dedication by Anna Magdalena Bach to Christiana Sibylla Bose

mit ihr befreundet – Anna Magdalena um 1741 den Predigtband der Betrachtungen über das gantze Leiden Christi von Johann Jacob Rambach (Jena 1732, 2. Auflage); sie tat das mit einer für sich sprechenden Widmung:

who was some ten years her junior and had become her friend, with a volume of sermons, the *Betrachtungen über das gantze Leiden Christi* (Contemplation of the Whole Suffering of Christ) by Johann Jacob Rambach (2nd edition Jena 1732); her inscription speaks for itself:

Als der HochEdlen, Hoch- Ehr- und Tugend= begabten Jonffer, Jonfer Christiana Sybilla Bosin, meiner besonders hochgeehrtesten Jonfer Gefatterin u. werthesten Hertzens Freündin erfreülcher Geburths Tag einfiel; wollte mit diesen kleinen doch wohl gemeinten Andencken sich bestens empfehlen. Anna Magdalena Bachin

"On the joyful birthday of the most noble, honorable, talented Christiana Sybilla Bosin, my most exemplary and honorable companion and bosom friend, I commend myself with this modest but well-meant token. Anna Magdalena Bach."

1744 wird die dann inzwischen 33-Jährige den Leipziger Kaufmann und Stadthauptmann Johann Zacharias Richter (1696–1764) heiraten. An zweiter Stelle ist als Pate M. Andreas Winckler (1684–1742) genannt (135). Von ihm ist außer einigen Lebensdaten wenig bekannt: In Leipzig geboren, besuchte er seit 1701 die Universität seiner Vaterstadt, wurde 1705 Magister der Philosophie und studierte in der Folge auch Theologie. In dem genannten Jahr trat er dem sogenannten *Donnerstägigen Prediger-Collegium* als Mitglied bei, das seit 1640 besteht und dessen Senior er 1715 wird. Später wurde er auch Mitglied des einst von August Hermann Francke gegründeten *Collegium Philobiblicum*. Im Dorf Starsiedel, südwestlich von Leipzig bzw. südlich von Lützen, besaß er das Rittergut und übte das Patrimonialrecht aus. Er besaß eine außergewöhnlich große eigene Bibliothek, die nach seinem Tode (19. April 1742) vom 3. September an im Roten Kolleg, dem Vaporarium, der Leipziger Universität versteigert wurde. Bei dieser Gelegenheit erstand Johann Sebastian für zehn Taler ein Exemplar der zehnbändigen Altenburger Luther-Ausgabe (1661–1663) aus dem Besitz Wincklers, über

In 1744, Christiana, then 33 years of age, married the Leipzig merchant and captain of the military guard, Johann Zacharias Richter (1696–1764). The second godparent was M. Andreas Winckler (1684–1742) (line 135). Apart from a few dates little is known about him. Born in Leipzig, he attended the university there from 1701 onward, received the master of philosophy degree in 1705, and then studied theology. In 1705 he joined the so-called *Thursday Preachers' Council* that existed since 1640 and whose chair he became in 1715. Later he also became a member of the *Collegium Philobiblicum*, founded by August Hermann Francke. He was patrimonial lord of the manor at in the village of Starsiedel, situated in the southwest of Leipzig and south of Lützen. He owned an unusually large library which was auctioned off after his death (April 19, 1742) in the "Red College", the university Vaporarium beginning on September 3. On that occasion Johann Sebastian Bach purchased a copy of the ten-volume Altenburg Luther edition (1661–1663) for ten thaler, for which he wrote an unusually detailed receipt.[35] He had seen the names of the previous

deren Erwerb er eine außergewöhnlich ausführliche Quittung[35] ausstellte. Denn er hatte auf den ersten Blättern die Namensvermerke von Vorbesitzern gelesen, die ihn offenbar besonders stolz auf seinen neuen Besitz machten:

owners on the first pages of the book, which made him particularly proud of his new acquisition:

Diese Teütsche und herrliche Schrifften des seeligen D. M. *Lutheri*, (so aus des großen *Wittenbergischen General-Superintendent*ens u. *Theologi D. Abrah: Calovii Bibliothec*, u. woraus Er vermuthlig seine große Teütsche *Bibel colligiret*; so auch nach deßen Absterben in des gleichfals großen *Theologi D. J. F. Mayers* Hände kommen) habe in einer *auction* erstanden *pro* 10 thl. a[nn]o 1742. *mense Septembris*.
Joh: Sebast: Bach.

"I purchased these wonderful German writings of the blessed D. Martin Luther in September 1742 at an auction for 10 Thaler. They came from the library of the esteemed Wittenberg superintendent and theologian D. Abraham Calovius, who undoubtedly used them for the edition of his great German Bible. After his death they came into the possession of the great theologian D. J. F. Mayer. Joh. Sebast. Bach."

Diese Quittung gibt nicht nur Aufschluss über Bachs Bevorzugung von Lutherschriften, sondern vermittelt auch seine Kenntnis von wichtigen zeitgenössischen Theologen, verbunden mit einem klaren Urteil über sie, und über die Tatsache, dass der Wittenberger Theologieprofessor Abraham Calov (1612–1686) exakt dieses Exemplar der Altenburger Lutherausgabe zur Kommentierung seiner großen Bibel benutzt hatte, der sogenannten

This receipt provides not only information about Bach's fondness for Luther's writings, but also shows his familiarity with important contemporary theologians, and his informed judgements about them. It also suggests that Abraham Calov (1612–1686), professor of theology in Wittenberg, had in fact used this copy of the Altenburg Luther edition for his great annotated Bible, the so-called "Calov Bible," which Bach also owned. Bach

„Calov-Bibel", die Bach ebenfalls besaß. Bach konnte das nur wissen, wenn er die Vorrede Calovs zu seiner mit Lutherschriften kommentierten Bibel aufmerksam gelesen hatte. Der andere genannte Wittenberger Theologe Johann Friedrich Mayer (1650–1712) wirkte später nach Jahren in Hamburg vor allem in Greifswald als Prediger an St. Nikolai, als Generalsuperintendent für Pommern und Rügen, als Präsident des Konsistoriums, *Professor Theologiae Primarius* sowie als Prokanzler der Universität Greifswald. Mayers Sohn versteigerte die für damalige Verhältnisse riesige Bibliothek seines Vaters von 18.000 Bänden 1716 in Berlin. Dort muss die Lutherausgabe in die Hände des Vorbesitzers Bachs, eben jenes Andreas Winckler, gekommen sein, aus dessen Bestand Bach sie 1742 kaufte. Als dritte Patin fungierte die Ehefrau M. Johann Christian Hebenstreits (1686–1756), des Konrektors der Thomasschule und Professors für Hebräische Sprache bei der Universität (136–139), Christiana Dorothea Hebenstreit (1709–1761). Sie war eine Tochter des Archidiakons von St. Nikolai und späteren Thomaspastors Friedrich Wilhelm Schütz (1677–1739), eines Großneffen des einstigen Dresdner Hofkapellmeisters Heinrich Schütz (1585–1672).

could only know this from carefully reading the preface of Calov's Bible, in which the author mentioned specific writings of Luther. The other Wittenberg theologian mentioned by Bach, Johann Friedrich Mayer (1650–1712), spent some years in Hamburg before becoming pastor at St. Nikolai in Greifswald, where he also served as general superintendent of Pomerania and Rügen, president of the church council, and *Professor Theologiae Primarius* (Senior Professor of Theology), as well as as vice chancellor of the University of Greifswald. In 1716 Mayer's son auctioned off his father's enormous library of 18.000 volumes in Berlin. At that auction the Altenburg Luther edition must have come into the hands of the owner preceding Bach, Andreas Winckler, from whose collection Bach bought it in 1742.
The third godparent was Christiana Dorothea Hebenstreit (1709–1761), wife of M. Johann Christian Hebenstreit (1686–1756), deputy rector of the St. Thomas School and professor of Hebrew at the university (lines 136–139). Christiana was the daughter of Friedrich Wilhelm Schütz (1677–1739), archdeacon of St. Nikolai and later pastor at St. Thomas, a greatnephew of the Dresden court capellmeister Heinrich Schütz (1585–1672).

Taufzettel 8
Im Jahr 1732 wurde **Johann Christoph Friedrich** (1732–1795) geboren. Er war das neunte Kind zweiter Ehe, geboren in Leipzig am 21. Juni, eine Woche nach dem Durchzug einer großen Gruppe Salzburger Exulanten (14.–16.6.1732) und reichlich zwei Wochen nach der feierlichen Einweihung der erneuerten Thomasschule (5. Juni 1732), zu der Bachs Kantate „Froher Tag, verlangte Stunden" (BWV Anh.18) aufgeführt wurde. Seine Mutter hatte erst zwei Monate vor seiner Geburt den aufwendigen Umzug aus der Interimswohnung des Hauses von Dr. Donndorf in der Hainstraße in die sanierte Wohnung der Thomasschule bewältigen müssen. Nun brachte sie einen Sohn zur Welt, aber nur reichlich zwei Monate später starb das im Jahr zuvor geborene Kind, Christiana Dorothea (Taufzettel 7), im Alter von nur 18 Monaten. Dass Anna Magdalena gegen Ende September Johann Sebastian zur Orgelprüfung nach Kassel begleiten würde, wird unter der Bedingung erfolgt sein, dass zu Hause mit der 24-jährigen Catharina Dorothea Bach, der ältesten der Geschwister, jemand die Verantwortung insbesondere für die vier jüngeren Kinder – neben dem inzwischen 3 Monate alten Johann Christoph Friedrich die Geschwister Gottfried Heinrich, inzwischen 8 Jahre alt, Elisabeth Juliana Friederica, 6 Jahre alt, Regina Johanna, reichlich 3 ½ Jahre alt – übernehmen konnte.

Baptismal Slip 8
Johann Christoph Friedrich (1732–1795) was born in Leipzig on June 21, 1732. The ninth child of the second marriage, he was born one week after a large group of Protestant refugees from Salzburg (June 14–16, 1732) had passed through Leipzig, and some two weeks after the festive opening ceremony of the renovated St. Thomas School (June 5, 1732). On that occasion Bach´s cantata "Froher Tag, verlangte Stunden" (BWV Anh.18) was performed. Some two months prior to Johann Christoph Friedrich's birth, Anna Magdalena had been caught up in the arduous move from the interim accommodations in Dr. Donndorf's house in Hainstraße to the refurbished apartment at the St. Thomas School. Two months after Johann Christoph Friedrich's birth, Christiana Dorothea (baptismal slip 7), born the year before, died at the age of 18 months. When toward the end of September Anna Magdalena accompanied her husband to an organ-examination in Kassel, the 24-year-old Catharina Dorothea Bach, the oldest of the siblings, assumed the responsibilities of the Bach household and especially cared for the four younger children – Gottfried Heinrich (8), Elisabeth Juliana Friederica (6), Regina Johanna (3 ½) and the three-month-old Johann Christoph Friedrich. Perhaps with this journey Johann Sebastian intended to give his overworked wife a chance to relax away

Vielleicht stand hinter der Mitreise auch der Gedanke Bachs, seiner stark belasteten Frau einmal eine Auszeit zu gönnen. Denn in Kassel wartete auf sie keinerlei Aufgabe. Allerdings erscheint es schon als eine mit Wagnissen behaftete Entscheidung, den dreimonatigen Säugling ohne Mutter zurückzulassen. Der Taufzettel zeigt wieder die gewohnte formularhafte saubere Gestalt in ausgeschriebener Kanzleischrift; lediglich der Name des Kindes (160) ist von Bach selbst eingetragen.

from home, as he had no real responsibilities in Kassel. Nonetheless, it was a risky decision to leave the three-month-old baby behind without his mother.

The baptismal slip shows the customary format in neat chancery hand; only the name of the baby (line 160) was inserted by Bach.

[8] *Leipzigk* 145
den 23 Junii 1732.
Des Kindes Vater ist Herr Johann Sebastian
Bach, Director Chori Musices und Cantor zu
St: Thomae alhier.
Die Mutter Frau Anna Magdalena gebohrne 150
Wilckin
Die Pathen sind
1 *HE. Johann Siegismund Beiche, Camer Comissarius*
und Amt=Mann in Pegau
2. *Jfr Dorothea* ~~Elisabeth~~ *Sophia, HE. D. Christian Weißens* 155
Pastoris zu St: Thomae alhier Jfr. Tochter
3. *HE. D. Christoph Donndorff, der Juristen Facultaet*
und des Fürstl. Merseburg. Land Gerichts in der
Nieder Lausitz Assessor.
Des Kindes Nahme Johann Christoph Friederich, etc. 160

$No \ \dfrac{29}{220} \ \mathfrak{D} \ H.\ M.\ G.$

[8]   Leipzigk
Juni 23, 1732.
The child's father is Mr Johann Sebastian
Bach, Director of Music and
Cantor at St. Thomas.
The mother is Anna Magdalena, née
Wilckin
The godparents are
1 Johann Siegismund Beiche, commissioner
   and bailiff in Pegau
2. Dorothea ~~Elisabeth~~ Sophia, daugther of
   D. Christian Weiß, pastor at St. Thomas.
3. Christoph Donndorff, assistant at the faculty of law
   and the Princely district court of Saxe-Merseburg in
   Lower Lusatia.
      The child's name is Johann Christoph Friederich, etc.

No $\dfrac{29}{220}$ ⟩ H. M. G.

Die Taufe vollzog Diaconus M. Gottlieb Gaudlitz (1694–1745) am Montag, dem 23. Juni 1732, Nachfolger Rabeners auf der dritten Pfarrstelle der Thomaskirche. Gelegentlich wurde vermutet, Gaudlitz habe unter pietistischen Einflüssen gestanden, weil er über dem Recht der Bestimmung der Gemeindelieder im Gottesdienst im Jahr 1728 mit Thomaskantor Bach in Streit geriet.[36] Doch lassen sein Lebenslauf und seine berufliche Karriere davon nichts erkennen: Gottlieb Gaudlitz stammte aus Leisnig, besuchte Schulen in Leipzig und Grimma, nahm 1713 das Studium an der Universität Leipzig auf, erwarb 1717 in Wittenberg die Magister-	The baptism was performed on Monday, June 23, 1732 by Deacon M. Gottlieb Gaudlitz, (1694–1745), Rabener's successor as third pastor at St. Thomas. It has been suggested that Gaudlitz was a Pietist, because in 1728 he became involved in an argument with Bach about who had the right to select the hymns for the church service.[36] But neither his curriculum vitae nor his professional career offer any hint of a Pietist disposition. Gottlieb Gaudlitz hailed from Leisnig, attended schools in Leipzig and Grimma, and began his university studies in Leipzig in 1713. In 1717 he was awarded the

Gottlieb Gaudlitz (1694–1745),
Pfarrer der Thomaskirche

Gottlieb Gaudlitz (1694–1745), pastor at St. Thomas

würde, war in Leipzig als Hauslehrer der Apelschen Kinder tätig und war Mitglied des großen donnerstägigen Prediger-Kollegiums an der Universitätskirche. Von 1721 an bekleidete er verschiedene geistliche Stellen an der Peterskirche, der Neuen Kirche, der Nikolaikirche und der Thomaskirche, wo er 1741 sogar das Pastorat erreichte; 1732 erwarb er an der Theologischen Fakultät den Licentiatentitel und wurde 1741 zum *Doctor Theologiae* promoviert. Doch bereits mit 51 Jahren segnete er das Zeitliche. Seit 1729 war er verheiratet. Von den bestellten Paten verweist der erste, Johann Siegismund Beiche

master's degree in Wittenberg and then worked as private tutor of the children of the Apel family in Leipzig, where he became a member of the Thursday Preachers' Council at the university church. After 1721 he occupied different ecclesiastical positions at St. Peter's, the Neue Kirche, the Nikolaikirche, and finally at St. Thomas, where he became pastor in 1741. In 1732 he had received the licentiate degree from the theological faculty, and in 1741 he was awarded the doctorate in theology. Married in 1729, he died at at the age of 51.
The first godparent, Johann Siegismund Beiche (of whom nothing is

(Lebensdaten unbekannt), auf die Beziehungen Bachs zum Stiftsland Naumburg-Zeitz. Es handelte sich bei Beiche um einen Amtmann aus Pegau, der zugleich Kammer-Kommissarius war. Womöglich hatte Bach diesen wenige Monate zuvor anlässlich seiner Orgelprüfung in Stöntzsch, nahe Pegau, kennengelernt. Später tauchte Beiche nochmals in Bachs Leben auf, indem er zum Mitinitiator der Huldigung für den Kammerherrn von Hennicke im Jahr 1737 in Wiederau wurde – unweit von Pegau und Stöntzsch ebenfalls im Zeitzer Stiftsland gelegen – wozu Bach seine Kantate „Angenehmes Wiederau" (BWV 30 a) komponierte.

Die als zweite Patin genannte Dorothea Sophia Weiß (1709–1751), die jüngere der beiden Töchter des Thomaspastors, heiratete sechs Jahre später den Universitätsprofessor Johann Erhard Kapp (1696–1756), der an der Philosophischen Fakultät Professor für Beredsamkeit war und als Vertrauter des Dresdner Superintendenten Valentin Ernst Löscher (1674–1749) in Leipzig[37] galt.

Der dritte Pate ist der bereits im Zusammenhang mit der Interimswohnung genannte Dr. jur. Christoph Donndorf (1667–1737). Er wird als Assessor der Juristenfakultät und des Fürstlich Merseburgischen Landgerichts in der Niederlausitz bezeichnet. Ihm gehörte jenes Haus in der Hainstraße, in welchem die Bachsche Familie für zehn Monate eine ausreichende Interimswohnung

known otherwise), points to Bach's relationship to the bishopric of Naumburg-Zeitz. Beiche was bailiff in Pegau and also held the post of tax commissioner. Perhaps Bach had met him several months earlier on the occasion of an organ examination in Stöntzsch near Pegau. Beiche appeared once again later in Bach's life when, in 1737, he was one of the initiators of the homage to the court chamberlain von Hennicke at Wiederau (situated near Pegau and Stöntzsch and belonging to the bishopric of Zeitz), prompting Bach to compose his cantata "Angenehmes Wiederau" (BWV 30a). The second godparent, Dorothea Sophia Weiß (1709–1751), was the younger of the two daughters of the pastor at St. Thomas. She married the university professor Johann Erhard Knapp (1696–1756), who was professor of eloquence at the philosophical faculty. Knapp was considered the close Leipzig confidant of the Dresden superintendent Valentin Ernst Löscher (1674–1749).[37]

The third godparent was Christoph Donndorf (1667–1737), doctor of jurisprudence, mentioned earlier in connection with the interim accommodations for the Bach family while their official residence was being renovated. Donndorf was assistant at the faculty of law and the district court of Merseburg in Lower Lusatia. He owned the house on Hainstraße which the Bach family took for ten months during the renovation of the Thomasschule in 1731/32. This

während des Thomasschulumbaus 1731/1732 zugewiesen bekam. Es handelte sich um das Haus Nr. 17 – seit 1850 unter dem Hausnamen „Lederhof" geführt –, das nach 1918 abgebrochen wurde und dessen Grundstück heute zusammengefügt ist mit dem Grundstück Nr. 19, seit dem frühen 17. Jahrhundert bis 1914 als „Haus zum goldnen Hahn" bezeichnet. Die Wohnung hatte zwei Vorteile: Für den Stadtrat war die Miete 15 Taler günstiger als die zur Auswahl angebotene im Haus des Dr. Packbusch am Brühl; außerdem war es für Bach näher zum Ausweichquartier des Alumnats und der Schule, welches sich im Kochischen Haus am Markt befand.

Auf der Rückseite des Taufzettels sind neben dem Namen des Bachsohnes vier weitere Namen vermerkt: Johann Gotthelff, Johann Christian, Johanna Regina, Johann Andreas. Ob es sich – wie früher schon vermutet – um weitere Mittäuflinge des Taufgottesdienstes am Montag, dem 23. Juni 1732 handelte, bleibt leider ungewiss.

Musikalisch-biografisch ist zu Johann Christoph Friedrich inzwischen eine Menge von wichtigen Einzelnachrichten aufgearbeitet. Er ist als „Bückeburger Bach" bekannt. Nach unbestätigten Mitteilungen habe er 1749 mit dem Studium der Rechtswissenschaften in Leipzig begonnen, dieses aber wegen des kritischen Gesundheitszustandes seines Vaters abgebrochen und Anfang des Jahres 1750 eine Stelle als

house – number 17 – since 1850 was known as "Leather Court"; it was demolished after 1918, when the property was joined with number 19, known from the early 17th century until 1914 as the "House of the Golden Rooster". Donndorf's apartment had two advantages: The rent, which was paid by the town council, was 15 thaler lower than that of an apartment offered in the house of Dr. Packbusch in the Brühl neighborhood; and besides, Donndorf's apartment was closer to the temporary boarding quarters for the boys and the school, located in Koch's house in the market square.

On the reverse side of the baptismal slip appear four names in addition to Bach´s infant son – Johann Gotthelff, Johann Christian, Johanna Regina and Johann Andreas. Unfortunately, it remains uncertain whether these were – as was assumed in the past – the names of other children also to be baptized during the service on Monday, June 23, 1732.

Today we have a great deal of important musical and biographical information regarding Johann Christoph Friedrich Bach. He is known as the "Bückeburg Bach". According to unconfirmed sources, he began to study law in Leipzig in 1749. However, the precarious state of his father's health prompted him to abandon his studies and in early 1750 assume the position of chamber musician of Count Wilhelm of

Kammermusiker beim Grafen Wilhelm von Schaumburg-Lippe (1724–1777) angenommen. Dort heiratete er im Januar 1755 die Sängerin Lucia Elisabeth Münchhausen (1728–1803), die Tochter eines Hofmusikers. Aus dieser Ehe gingen neun Kinder hervor, von denen nur fünf erwachsen wurden: Anna Philippina Friederica (1755–1804) – ihre Nachkommen leben in der Familie Colson heute noch –, Wilhelm Friedrich Ernst (1759–1845), Christina Luisa (1762–1852), Carolina Wilhelmine (1765–1852) und Dorothea Charlotte Magdalena (1772–1793). Als Johann Gottfried Herder (1744–1803) im Jahr 1771 als Hofprediger und Konsistorialrat nach Bückeburg kam, entwickelte sich nicht nur eine Freundschaft zwischen beiden, sondern auch eine Arbeitsgemeinschaft für Oratorien, Kantaten und dramatische Werke. Nach fünf Jahren ging Herder jedoch nach Weimar; auch starb die Gräfin von Schaumburg-Lippe und im Jahr darauf auch der Graf. In diesem Tief muss es ihm wie eine helfende Hand erschienen sein, dass er 1778 zusammen mit seinem achtzehnjährigen Sohn eine Reise nach London unternehmen konnte, auf der er seine Brüder Carl Philipp Emanuel in Hamburg und Johann Christian in London besuchte. Der Nachfolger Herders in Bückeburg, Karl Gottlieb Horstig (1763–1835), lobt im Nekrolog Bachs „Rechtschaffenheit, Seelengröße, Dienstfertigkeit und Gefälligkeit".

Schaumburg-Lippe (1724–1777). In January 1755 he married the singer Lucia Elisabeth Münchhausen (1728–1803), the daughter of a court musician. Nine children, of whom only five reached adulthood, came from this marriage: Anna Philippina Friederica (1755–1804) – her descendants are still found today in the family Colson – Wilhelm Friedrich Ernst (1759–1845), Christina Luisa (1762–1852), Carolina Wilhelmine (1765–1852) and Dorothea Charlotte Magdalena (1772–1793). When Johann Gottfried Herder (1744–1803) settled in Bückeburg in 1771 as court preacher and councillor of the consistory, he and Johann Christoph Friedrich became friends and the two collaborated on oratorios, cantatas, and other dramatic works. Five years later Herder moved to Weimar, however; then the countess of Schaumburg-Lippe died, and a year later her husband. In this time of melancholy it must have been a blessing to Johann Christoph Friedrich to be able to undertake a journey with his eighteen-year-old son (in 1778) to visit his brothers Carl Philipp Emanuel in Hamburg and Johann Christian in London. Herder's successor in Bückeburg, Karl Gottlieb Horstig (1763–1835), praised Bach in his obituary for his "honesty, dignity of soul, readiness to be of service and courtesy."
From none other than his mother came a unique testimony of her attachment to and affection for this particular

Gerade von der Hand seiner Mutter besitzen wir ein einzigartiges Zeugnis der Verbundenheit und Liebe zu diesem Sohn. Als bereits feststand, dass er Anfang des Jahres 1750 das Vaterhaus würde verlassen müssen, weil mit dem Angebot der Stelle in Bückeburg sich die berufliche Zukunft auch dieses Bachsohnes zu klären begann, schenkte seine Mutter ihm zum Weihnachtsfest eine Bibel. Es handelte sich um eine Handausgabe, gedruckt in Eisleben im Jahr 1736. Anderen Quellen zufolge wissen wir, dass es eine Handbibel war, die in Leipzig gleichsam kirchenamtlich weitergegeben wurde. Diese Bibel aus dem Eigentum Anna Magdalenas mit der Einprägung „A. M. B." und „1738" ist in der Staatsbibliothek Preußischer Kulturbesitz zu Berlin erhalten geblieben. Sie war von dem Eislebener Superintendenten Andreas Kunad (1675–1746) herausgegeben und von ihm mit einem bedeutsames Vorwort versehen worden. In diesem setzte Kunad sich kritisch mit den inzwischen stärker werdenden Forderungen nach einer grundsätzlichen sprachlichen Überarbeitung der Luther-Übersetzung der Bibel auseinander. Mit hohem Sachverstand beleuchtete er Versuche, den originalen Wortlaut der Luther-Bibel zu verändern, vor allem dort, wo es lediglich um die Anpassung ihrer Sprachform an den damals modernen Geschmack geht.

Auf dem Vorsatzblatt dieses Bibelexemplars befindet sich eine Widmung Anna Magdalena Bachs an ihren Sohn:

son. When it became evident that early in 1750 he would leave his parental home with the offer of a position in Bückeburg his professional future began to take shape, his mother's Christmas gift was a Bible. It was a pocket edition, printed in Eisleben in 1736. This Bible had been in the possession of Anna Magdalena and was inscribed with the initials "A. M. B." and the year "1738"; today it is housed at the Staatsbibliothek zu Berlin – Stiftung Preußischer Kulturbesitz. It was edited by Andreas Kunad (1675–1746), superintendent of Eisleben. In an important preface Kunad responded critically to the increasing demand for a fundamental linguistic revision of Luther's Bible translation. With considerable expertise he examined various attempts to change the original wording of Luther's Bible, especially the demand to accommodate Luther's language to modern idiom.

Anna Magdalena Bach's dedication to her son is found on the fly leaf of this Bible:

"I give this wonderful book, as a constant reminder and for true Christian edification to my beloved son. Anna Magdalena Bach née Wilckin. Your faithful and well-meaning mother. Leipzig, December 25, 1749." This testimony of love and affection becomes all the more significant because the Bible had been Anna Magdalena's personal possession; the imprint on the leather binding has

Bibel der Anna Magdalena mit Widmung an ihren Sohn, Titel und Frontispiz

Bible of Anna Magdalena with dedication to her son, title and frontispiece

> Zum steten Andencken
> und Christlicher erbau=
> ung schencket ihrem
> lieben Sohn dieses herliche
> Buch
> Anna Magdalena Bachin
> gebohrne Wülckin
> deine getreu und
> wohl meinde Mamma.
> Leipzig d 25 Decemb:
> 1749.

Dieses Zeugnis der Liebe und Zuneigung zu ihrem Sohn gewinnt an Besonderheit durch die Tatsache des nachweisbaren Eigentums dieser Bibel aus den Beständen Anna Magdalenas; die Einprägung auf dem Ledereinband wurde bereits erwähnt. Die Widmung schreibt sie ein im Bewusstsein des Abschieds des Sohnes vom Elternhaus, sie bestimmt die Bibel zur „Erbauung" und sie bezeichnet sie als „herliche[s] Buch". Das alles ist in der Lage, einen bestimmten Geist zu übermitteln, der im Hause Johann Sebastian Bachs geherrscht haben muss. Dazu passt schließlich auch die Übereignungsformel, die Treue und Wohlmeinen der Geberin mit auf den Weg gibt. Gerade darin mag sich nicht nur Charakteristisches Anna Magdalenas widerspiegeln, sondern auch ein bestimmtes Charakteristikum dieses Sohnes.

been already mentioned. She wrote her dedication with her son's leaving the parental home in mind, intending the Bible to be for his "edification" and describing it as a "wonderful book." All this conveys a sense of the spirit that must have prevailed in the house of Johann Sebastian Bach. This included the dedicatory words, which assured the writer's trust and benevolence – probably reflecting not only Anna Magdalena's disposition but that of her son as well.

Taufzettel 9

Wegen des Todes Augusts des Starken am 1. Februar wurde im Jahr 1733 eine knapp viermonatige Trauerzeit – *tempus clausum* – angeordnet, während der auch die Figuralmusik in den Kirchen zu schweigen hatte. Wir wissen, dass Bach die damit geschenkte Zeit sinnvoll nutzte. Allein in diesem Jahr entstanden mehrere Werke für das kurfürstliche Haus in Dresden. Zunächst war es die sogenannte Dresdner *Missa*, Kyrie und Gloria der späteren h-Moll-Messe (BWV 232 I), die Bach schrieb. Gelegentlich ist vermutet worden, Bach

Baptismal Slip 9

The death of the Saxon elector August the Strong on February 1, 1733 was followed by a period of mourning – *tempus clausum* – which lasted four months. No figured music was allowed in the churches during that time. We know that Bach used this time creatively. In that year alone he composed several works for the princely court in Dresden, beginning with the so-called Dresden *Mass* (BWV 232 I), i.e. the Kyrie and Gloria that later were incorporated into the B Minor Mass. It has occasionally been assumed that

habe diese beiden Messeteile bereits im Erbhuldigungsgottesdienst für den neuen sächsischen Kurfürsten Friedrich August II. (1696/1733–1763) am 21. April 1733 in der Nikolaikirche[38] aufgeführt, was aber gemäß der handschriftlich erhaltenen Gottesdienstordnung nicht der Fall war.[39] Kurz nach diesem Ereignis starb das Töchterchen Regina Johanna (vgl. Taufzettel 5) im Alter von 4 ½ Jahren und wurde am 26. April auf dem Johannisfriedhof beerdigt.[40] Seit Anfang Juli arbeiteten Bach selbst, Anna Magdalena und die älteren Söhne Wilhelm Friedemann und Carl Philipp Emanuel an der Reinschrift des Stimmensatzes der genannten Missa. Inzwischen hatte Bach die Wahl Wilhelm Friedemanns zum Organisten der Dresdner Sophienkirche durch entsprechende Briefe vorbereitet. Frühestens am 19., spätestens aber am Sonntag, 26. Juli 1733, reiste Bach mit seinem ältesten Sohn nach Dresden, um den Stimmensatz mit einem persönlichen Schreiben dem Kurfürsten überreichen zu lassen. Das Schreiben ist mit dem 27. Juli 33 datiert. Darin zeigt sich Bach zu Diensten erbötig und bittet um „ein *Praedicat* von Dero Hoff-*Capelle*". Wenige Tage später, am 1. August 1733, tritt Wilhelm Friedemann sein neues Amt in Dresden an. Kurz zuvor oder auch darauf muss Bach eilends wieder nach Leipzig zurückgekehrt sein, denn für den Namenstag des Kurfürsten am 3. August hatte er eine Kantate zur Aufführung durch

Bach gave a first performance of these two parts of the Mass already during the service held at the Nikolaikirche on April 21, 1733 to honor the new Saxon elector Friedrich August II (1696/1733–1763).[38] A look at the handwritten liturgy of the service reveals, however, that this cannot have been the case.[39] Shortly after this, Bach's young daughter Regina Johanna (baptismal slip no. 5) died at the age of 4 ½ years and was buried in the cemetery of St. Johannis on April 26.[40] Since early July Bach had worked together with Anna Magdalena and his older sons Wilhelm Friedemann and Carl Philipp Emanuel on preparing the performance materials of the *Missa*. In the meantime he had written a number of letters to bring about Wilhelm Friedemann's appointment as organist of the Dresden Sophienkirche. Sometime between July 19 and 26, Bach and his oldest son traveled to Dresden to present the set of parts and an accompanying letter to the Elector. Dated July 27, 1733, the letter expressed Bach's readiness to serve the elector and solicited the title of "Hof-Compositeur". A few days later, on August 1, Wilhelm Friedemann assumed his new position in Dresden. Bach evidently returned to Leipzig in a hurry, for by August 3 he had composed a cantata for the Elector's patron saint's day to be performed by the Collegium Musicum: "Frohes Volk, vergnügte Sachsen" (BWV Anh. 12). One month later, on September 5, the cantata

das Collegium musicum vorbereitet: „Frohes Volk, vergnügte Sachsen" (BWV Anh. 12). Einen Monat danach, am 5. September, erklingt zum Geburtstag des Kurprinzen die Kantate „Lasst uns sorgen, lasst uns wachen" (BWV 213). Und exakt drei Monate später führt Bach zum Geburtstag der Kurfürstin Maria Josepha (1699/1733–1757) die Kantate „Tönet, ihr Pauken! Erschallet Trompeten" (BWV 214) auf. Mit den beiden zuletzt genannten Kantaten hatte er Stücke geschrieben, die ihm im Folgejahr für die Komposition des Weihnachtsoratoriums zur Verfügung stehen würden.

Mitten in diesem dichten Ablauf beruflicher Obliegenheiten ihres Mannes – Planungen, Kompositionen, Vorbereitungen von Textdrucken, Herstellen der Aufführungsmaterialien, die weiterlaufenden gottesdienstlichen Verpflichtungen – bereitete Anna Magdalena sich auf die Geburt ihres zehnten Kindes vor. Wohl am 4. November bringt Anna Magdalena einen Knaben zu Welt, der am folgenden Tag in der Thomaskirche die heilige Taufe empfängt. Bach fügt dem mustergültig vorbereiteten Taufzettel zu der Formulierung „Des Kindes Nahme" hinzu „soll heisen **Johann, August, Abraham**. etc." (180–181). Es ist Donnerstag (183), und die Taufe wird in St. Thomas wohl nach dem morgendlichen Wochengottesdienst stattgefunden haben. Taufender Pfarrer ist Archidiaconus Lic. Urban Gottfried Sieber (1669–1741), zugleich außerordentlicher

"Lasst uns sorgen, lasst uns wachen" (BWV 213) was performed on the occasion of the Elector's birthday. And to the day three months later, Bach performed the cantata "Tönet, ihr Pauken! Erschallet Trompeten" (BWV 214) for the birthday of the Elector's wife, Maria Josepha (1699/1733–1757). These two cantatas included parts that he subsequently utilized for the composition of his Christmas Oratorio the following year.

In the midst of this intense sequence of her husband's professional responsibilities – planning, composing, preparing printed cantata texts, producing performance materials, not to mention his extensive church responsibilities – Anna Magdalena prepared for the birth of her tenth child. Probably on November 4, she was delivered a baby boy, who was baptized in St. Thomas the following day. Johann Sebastian Bach added to the formulation "The child's name shall be ... " on the properly prepared baptismal slip the names "**Johann, August, Abraham**, etc." (lines 180–181). It was a Thursday (line 183) and the baptism probably took place after the morning service at St. Thomas. The officiating pastor was Archdeacon Lic. Urban Gottfried Sieber (1669–1741), professor at the theological faculty. He had also baptized Gottfried Heinrich Bach (baptismal slip no. 1). Evidently, together with the Bachs' new baby, two other infants – named Johann Gottfried and Sophia Elisabeth (noted on the re-

Professor an der Theologischen Fakultät. Er war bereits Taufpfarrer von Gottfried Heinrich Bach (Taufzettel 1) gewesen. Mit dem Kind Bachs wurden offenbar noch zwei weitere Kinder namens Johann Gottfried und Sophia Elisabeth (vermerkt auf der Rückseite des Taufzettels) getauft; jedenfalls handelte es sich um die fünfte Taufe im Monat November und die 362. im laufenden Jahr.

verse of the baptismal slip) – were also baptized, and this was the fifth baptism in November and the 362nd of the year.

[9]
Leipzigk den 5 Nov:
1733.
Des Kindes Vater ist Herr Johann
Sebastian Bach, Director Chori Musici
und Cantor zu St: Thomae.
Die Mutter Frau Anna Magdalena
gebohrne Wilckin
Die Pathen sind

1. HE. M. Johann August Ernest, bey der
Schulen zu St: Thomae Con=Rector alhier
 2 1
2. Fr. Charitas Elisabeth, HE. M. Johann
Matthiae Geßners, Rectoris bey der Schulen
zu St: Thomae alhier Fr. Eheliebste

3. HE. M. Abraham Kriegel, Collega Tertius
bey der Schulen zu St: Thomae alhier.

Des Kindes Nahme soll heisen
Johann, August, Abraham, etc.

No $\frac{5}{362}$ 4   H. L. S.

[9]   Leipzig, November 5,
       1733.
The child's father is Johann
   Sebastian Bach, Director of the Musical Choirs
   And Cantor at St. Thomas.
   The mother is Anna Magdalena
         née Wilckin
         The godparents are

1. M. Johann August Ernest, conrector at St. Thomas
   here in Leipzig.
         2   1
2. Charitas Elisabeth, dearest wife of M. Johann
   Matthias Geßner, Rector at
   St. Thomas

3. M. Abraham Kriegel, Collega Tertius
   at St. Thomas School here in Leipzig.

         The child's name is
         Johann, August, Abraham, etc.

   No $\frac{5}{362}$ 4   H. L. S.

Die Paten bittet Bach diesmal sämtlich aus dem Bereich der Kollegenschaft der Thomasschule: An erster Stelle handelt es sich um den Konrektor M. Johann August Ernesti (1707–1781), einen ehrgeizigen und damals noch jungen Mann von 26 Jahren, der eine glänzende Karriere begonnen hatte.

Der gebürtige Superintendentensohn Johann August Ernesti aus Tennstedt

Bach chose the godparents from among his colleagues at the St. Thomas School. The first godparent was the conrector M. Johann August Ernesti (1707–1781), an ambitious young man of 26 years, who had just commenced a brilliant career.

Born in Tennstädt, the son of Superintendent Johann August Ernesti, he had at this point taught at the St.

Johann August Ernesti
(1707–1781), Konrektor,
später Rektor der Thomasschule

Johann August Ernesti
(1707–1781), Deputy Rector,
later Rector of the
St. Thomas School

war zu dieser Zeit erst seit zwei Jahren an der Thomasschule tätig. Nach dem Besuch der Fürstenschule von Schulpforta (1723–1726) und der Universität Wittenberg (1726–1728) kam er an die Universität Leipzig, wo er bereits am 16. Februar 1730 seine Magisterpromotion verteidigte. Auf Empfehlung seines Portenser Rektors, Friedrich Gotthilf Freytag, wurde er anschließend Hauslehrer der Kinder des Leipziger Bürgermeisters Christian Ludwig Stieglitz

Thomas School for two years. After attending the Princely School of Schulpforta (1723–1726) and the University of Wittenberg (1726–1728), he studied at the University of Leipzig, where he received his master's degree on February 16, 1730. On recommendation of his headmaster at Schulpforta, Friedrich Gotthilf Freytag, he became private tutor of the children of the Leipzig mayor Christian Ludwig Stieglitz (1677–1758),

(1677–1758), seit 1729 Vorsteher der Thomasschule. Nach dem Tod des 76-jährigen Rektors Johann Heinrich Ernesti 1729 und dem des designierten Konrektors Carl Friedrich Petzold im Jahr 1731 war es – sicher auf Betreiben Stieglitz' – zu einem Generationswechsel in der Leitung der Schule gekommen. Der neue Rektor, Johann Matthias Gesner, kam mit 39 Jahren nach Leipzig und setzte sich 1731 für den streng philologisch arbeitenden Gräzisten, eben den jüngeren Ernesti, ausdrücklich ein, der aus einer Gruppe von weiteren sieben Bewerbern ausgewählt wurde, nachdem er einen deutschen Text ins Lateinische und Griechische übersetzt und kommentiert hatte. Ernestis Ehrgeiz ließ zunächst auch familiäre Absichten – er heiratete erst 1743 Rahel Friederike Amalie Dathe aus Weißenfels, die bald wieder verstarb – hintanstehen; 1742 trat er eine außerordentliche Professur der *litterae humaniores* an der Philosophischen Fakultät der Universität an, der 1756 die Beförderung auf eine Professur der Beredsamkeit folgte, bevor er nach Erwerb der theologischen Doktorwürde schließlich 1759 Professor der Theologie wurde. Noch herrschte aufgrund der erstaunlichen Führungsqualität Gesners ein nie da gewesenes Einvernehmen unter den Lehrerpersönlichkeiten, was sich auch in der Wahl der zweiten Patin ausdrückt: Elisabeth Charitas Gesner, geborene Eberhardt (1695–1761), war eine

who since 1729 was rector of the St. Thomas School. After the rector Johann Heinrich Ernesti had died in 1729 at the age of 76, followed in 1731 by the designated conrector Carl Friedrich Petzold, it was probably Stieglitz, who instigated a generational change in the administration of the school. The new rector, Johann Matthias Gesner, came to Leipzig at the age of 39 and in 1731 resolutely opted for the younger Ernesti, a strictly philologically oriented Greek scholar; he was selected from a list of seven applicants after translating a German text into both Latin and Greek and subsequently providing an erudite commentary. His career appears to have been more important to Ernesti at first than his private life: He was married only in 1743 – to Rahel Friederike Amalie Dathe from Weißenfels, who died soon after, however. In 1742 he became associate professor of *litterae humaniores* in the Faculty of Philosophy at Leipzig University and in 1756 advanced to professor of eloquence; in 1759 finally he was made professor of theology after being awarded the doctorate in this discipline. Gesner's striking leadership qualities at first led to an unprecedented harmonious relationship among the teachers of the school, which also found expression in Bach's choice of the second godparent: Elisabeth Charitas Gesner, née Eberhardt (1695–1761),

Pfarrerstochter aus Geraberg in Thüringen, seit 1718 mit Johann Matthias Gesner (1691–1761) verheiratet. Bach und Gesner mussten sich schon in Weimar begegnet sein, wo Gesner seit 1715 Konrektor des Gymnasiums, Verwalter der Herzoglichen Bibliothek und des Münzkabinetts gewesen war. Als er nach dem Tod des Weimarer Herzogs Wilhelm Ernst 1728 alle Nebenämter verlor, übernahm er für kurze Zeit das Rektorat in Ansbach. Doch schon von Weimar aus war er oftmals Gast bei dem Leipziger Buchhändler und Verleger Thomas Fritzsch (1666–1726) gewesen und hatte an der „Dienstagsgesellschaft" teilgenommen, wo er einflussreichen Persönlichkeiten wie Christian Ludwig Stieglitz (1677–1758), Leonhard Baudiß († 1733), Johann Burchard Mencke (1675–1732) und Johann Jacob Mascow (1689–1761) begegnet war. Diese sorgten für seine Berufung als Nachfolger des älteren Ernesti. Doch bereits Mitte des Jahres 1734 reichte er beim Leipziger Stadtrat die Bitte um Entlassung ein, da er eine Berufung als Professor der Philologie an die neu gegründete Universität Georgia-Augusta in Göttingen erhalten hatte.

Zum dritten Paten bat Bach seinen Lehrerkollegen auf dem Tertiat der Thomasschule M. Abraham Kriegel (1691–1759).

Abraham Kriegel wurde 1691 in Volkersdorf in Schlesien geboren und erhielt 1725 die Stelle des Quartus an der Leipziger Thomasschule. Kurz darauf heiratete er Christiana

daughter of a pastor from Geraberg in Thuringia and since 1718 married to Johann Matthias Gesner (1691–1761). Bach and Gesner must have met already in Weimar, where Gesner had been appointed conrector of the secondary school in 1715 as well as curator of the ducal library and the ducal medal collection. When he lost the latter offices after the death of Duke Wilhelm Ernst in 1728, he briefly became rector of the school in Ansbach. Even while in Weimar he had frequently been a guest of the Leipzig bookseller and publisher Thomas Fritzsch (1666–1726), and had participated in the "Tuesday Society," where he had met such influential individuals as Christian Ludwig Stieglitz (1677–1758), Leonhard Baudiß (†1733), Johann Burchard Mencke (1675–1732), and Johann Jacob Mascow (1689–1761). These men saw to his appointment as the older Ernesti's successor. However, already in mid-1734 Gesner requested the Leipzig city council to release him from his obligations as he had received a professorship in philology at the newly founded Georgia-Augusta University in Göttingen.

As third godparent Bach asked a colleague at the St. Thomas School, M. Abraham Kriegel (1691–1759).

Kriegel was born in 1691 in Volkersdorf (Silesia) and in 1725 took up the position of *Quartus*, or fourth teacher, at the St. Thomas School. Soon thereafter he married Christiana Charlotte, née Hänisch. After the de-

Abraham Kriegel, Nützliche Nachrichten, 1752

Abraham Kriegel, Useful News, 1752

Charlotte, geborene Hänisch. Nach dem Abgang des Konrektors Hebenstreit zur Universität erhielt Kriegel die Stelle des Tertius. Im Zusammenhang mit dem plötzlichen Tod des designierten Konrektors Petzold bewarb auch Kriegel sich um das Konrektorat, blieb aber nach der Wahl des jüngeren Ernesti Tertius. Anfang Juli 1732 starb seine erste Frau[41]. Ende November 1735 heiratete er die Pfarrerstochter Johanna Charlotta, geborene Wendt, aus Collmen bei Leisnig. Bach war zu dieser Hochzeit zusammen mit Johann August Ernesti nach Collmen eingeladen.[42]

parture of the conrector Hebenstreit, who went to the university, Kriegel advanced to the position of *Tertius*. After the sudden death of the designated conrector Petzold, Kriegel, too, applied for this position but had to continue as *Tertius* when the younger Ernesti was appointed. Kriegel's first wife died in early July of 1732.[41] In late November 1735, he married Johanna Charlotta, née Wendt, daughter of the parish pastor of Collmen near Leisnig. Bach was invited to this wedding together with Johann August Ernesti.[42] Kriegel had one son, Christian August Kriegel, who

Aus dieser Ehe ging ein Sohn hervor, Christian August Kriegel, der bis 1803 als Quartus an der Thomasschule tätig war. Abraham Kriegel machte sich verdient mit der Herausgabe der „Nützliche[n] Nachrichten von denen Bemühungen derer Gelehrten und anderen Begebenheiten in Leipzig", die in den Jahren von 1739 bis 1756 erschienen. Leider verstarb der Knabe bereits nach zwei Tagen[43] und am 7. November folgte seine Beerdigung auf dem Johannisfriedhof östlich der Stadt.

Taufzettel 10
Am Montag nach dem 13. Sonntag nach Trinitatis, dem 5. September 1735, wurde Anna Magdalena von ihrem elften Kind entbunden. Es war ein Junge, der zwei Tage später, am Mittwoch, dem 7. September, in der Thomaskirche – wahrscheinlich vormittags – durch Archidiakon Lic. Urban Gottfried Sieber (1669–1741) die heilige Taufe empfing und den Namen **Johann Christian** (1735–1782) erhielt. Der Taufzettel ist wieder in gewohnter Akkuratheit vorbereitet, doch neben dem eigenen Eintrag des Kindesnamens fühlte sich Johann Sebastian Bach bemüßigt, verschiedentlich mit Änderungen einzugreifen: Zuerst ist es die Bezeichnung seines Kapellmeistertitels. Noch auf dem Taufzettel der Nottaufe von Regina Johanna im Oktober 1728, den er selbst vollständig geschrieben hatte, bezeichnete er sich als „Hochf. Anh. Cöthenischer Capell-

taught as *Quartus* at the St. Thomas School until 1803.
Between 1739 and 1756 Abraham Kriegel published his *Nützliche Nachrichten von den Bemühungen derer Gelehrten und anderen Begebenheiten in Leipzig*.
Sadly, the infant boy died after only two days; his burial followed on November 7 at the cementry of St. Johannis situated east of the town.[43]

Baptismal Slip 10
On the Monday following the 13th Sunday after Trinity – September 5, 1735 – Anna Magdalena gave birth to her eleventh child, a boy. **Johann Christian** (1735–1782) was baptized two days later, on Wednesday, September 7, – probably in the morning – in St. Thomas by Archdeacon Lic. Urban Gottfried Sieber (1669–1741). The baptismal slip was again prepared with the customary accuracy, but next to his entry of the child's name, Johann Sebastian Bach felt obliged to make several modifications. The first had to do with his title as capellmeister. On the baptismal slip of Regina Johanna's emergency baptism in October 1728, written entirely by himself, he had described himself as "Capellmeister of the Prince of Anhalt-Cöthen, as well as *Director Chori Musici Lipsiensis* and cantor at St. Thomas". As this title had

meister, wie auch Director Chori Musici Lipsiensis u. Cantor zu S. Thomae"; nun da mit dem Tod des Fürsten Leopold von Anhalt-Köthen am 19. November 1728 dieser Titel erloschen war, hatte er im Februar 1729 durch Herzog Christian (1682–1736) den Titel eines Weißenfelsischen Kapellmeisters erhalten. Auffällig ist sodann die Veränderung der Reihenfolge der Paten durch Umnummerierung; der Schreiber hatte als ersten Paten den Thomasschulrektor Ernesti, als zweite Patin die Bose-Tochter von gegenüber und als dritten Paten den Rechtsprofessor Rivinus genannt. Ausdrücklich werden durch Korrektur der Ziffern die beiden männlichen Paten zu 1 und 3 ausgetauscht. Ein Blick in das Taufbuch der Thomaskirche, das eigentlich die als endgültig zu betrachtenden Angaben des Taufzettels übernehmen sollte, zeigt aber die alte Reihenfolge. Nicht feststellbar ist, ob Bach der Schreiber der veränderten Nummerierung ist. Außerdem fügte Bach dem Namen „Ernest" ein „i" hinzu und strich wohl auch den überflüssigen Assessorentitel bei dem Paten Rivinus aus. Eine weitere Handschrift zeigt sich bei den Registriernummern, die ebenfalls verändert wurden, aus 11 zu 12 (Taufen im Monat November) und aus 313 zu 314 (Taufen im Jahr 1735; ebenso auf der Rückseite des Zettels), einschließlich dem Vermerk zum Wochentag (Mittwoch) und dem Taufpfarrer Sieber, der bereits bei den Taufen 1 und 9 begegnete.

lapsed with the death of prince Leopold of Coethen-Anhalt on November 19, 1728, in February 1729 he had received from Duke Christian (1682–1736) the title of a capellmeister of Weißenfels. Next we notice the change in the sequence of the godparents, through the shift in numbering; the writer had originally named the rector of the St. Thomas School, Ernesti, as the first godparent, Bose's daughter from the neighboring house as second Godparent, and Rivinus as third. The order of the two male godparents was changed deliberately by reversing the numbers 1 and 3. An examination of the baptismal register of St. Thomas, which generally is supposed to take over the details of the baptismal slip in their exact form, still indicated the old sequence, however. It is not clear if Bach was the writer of the changed numbering. In addition, Bach added an "i" to the name "Ernest" and probably also crossed out the superfluous title of "assessor" for the godparent Rivinus. Yet another hand wrote the registration numbers, which also had to be altered – from 11 to 12 (baptisms in the month of November) and from 313 to 314 (baptisms in the year 1735; see also the reverse side of the slip) – as well as the day of the week (Wednesday) and the officiating cleric, Pastor Sieber, who had also attended baptisms nos. 1 and 9.

[10]
                Leipzig
              den 7 Septemb:
                 1735.
Des Kindes Vater ist Herr Johann Sebastian
  Bach, hochfürstl. ~~Cöthenisch.~~ Weißenfels. Capell Meister, Director
  Chori Musici und Cantor zu St Thomae
Die Mutter Frau Anna Magdalena gebohrne
      Wilckin
    Die Pathen sind
[1] (3 Herr M. Johann August Ernesti, Rector zu
     St: Thomae alhier

    (2. Jfr. Christiana Sibylla, H. George Heinrich
       Bosens, Kauff und Handelsmanns
       alhier nachgel. Jfr. Tochter

[3] (1 Herr D. Johann Florens Rivinus, Jctus. P. P.
     des Concilii Profess: ~~Assessor~~ wie auch der
     Juristen Facultaet Assessor alhier

         Des Kindes Nahme.
         Johann Christian.

No $\dfrac{12}{314}$ ☿   H. L. Sieber.

---

[10]
                Leipzig
              September 7,
                1735.
The child's father is Johann Sebastian
  Bach, Princely ~~Cöthen-~~ Weissenfels capellmeister, Director
  Chori Musici and Cantor at St. Thomas.
The mother is Anna Magdalena née
      Wilckin
    The godparents are
[1] (3 M. Johann August Ernesti, Rector
     at St. Thomas

(2. Christiana Sibylla, daugter of
George Heinrich Bose,
merchant.

[3] (1 D. Johann Florens Rivinus, Jctus. P. P. of the Council,
professor ~~assessor~~, as well as
in the faculty of law

200

The child's name shall be
Johann Christian.

No $\dfrac{12}{314}$ ☿   H. L. Sieber.

205

Offensichtlich gab es das ausdrückliche Interesse Bachs an der Übernahme der ersten Patenstelle durch den Juristen Johann Florens Rivinus (1681–1755), von dessen Familie bereits früher (vgl. Taufzettel 1) die Rede war. Johann Florens Rivinus stammte aus einer verzweigten Leipziger Mediziner-, Theologen- und Juristenfamilie. Seit 1704 in erster Ehe verheiratet mit seiner Kusine Clara Susanne Rivinus (1686–1739), wurde er Mitte des Jahres 1723 zum ordentlichen Professor der Leipziger Juristenfakultät berufen, wozu vermutlich Bach ihm bereits eine Glückwunschkantate komponierte, „Murmelt nur, ihr heitern Bäche" (BWV deest). Er vereinte viele Ehrenämter: Dekan des Domstifts Wurzen, Domherr zu Merseburg, Erbherr auf Neumuckershausen und

Bach obviously had a special interest in giving the primacy of place among the godparents to the lawyer Johann Florens Rivinus (1681–1755), whose family has already been mentioned (see baptismal slip no. 1).

Johann Florens Rivinus came from a distinguished Leipzig family with many physicians, theologians and lawyers. In 1704 he married his cousin Clara Susanne Rivinus (1686–1739). He was appointed professor of law in Leipzig in the summer of 1723, whereupon Bach may have composed the congratulatory cantata, "Murmelt nur, ihr heitern Bäche" (BWV deest). Rivinus came to hold numerous honorary offices: dean of Wurzen cathedral, member of the Chapter of Merseburg cathedral, hereditary lord of Neumuckershausen, and member of the Council of Ten at the university,

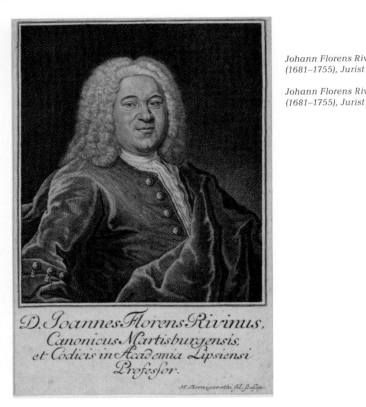

Johann Florens Rivinus
(1681–1755), Jurist

Johann Florens Rivinus
(1681–1755), Jurist

Decemvir der Universität; 1729 übernahm er erstmalig deren Rektorat. Nun – gerade im Jahr 1735 – schickte er sich an, dieses erneut anzutreten. Verschwägert mit den Familien der Theologen Olearius und der Juristen Graff, ergibt sich über ihn sogar eine verwandtschaftliche Verbindung zur Familie Georg Friedrich Händels nach Halle/S. Mit seinem Namen verbindet sich auch die Einrichtung der Glückwunschkantate „Die Freude reget sich" (BWV 36b), fünfte und

whose rector he became for the first time in 1729, assuming that office for a second time six years later, in 1735. He was related by marriage to the families of the theologian Olearius and the lawyer Graff, and there was also a distant relationship to the family of Georg Friedrich Händel in Halle. Rivinus' name is associated with the composition of the congratulatory cantata "Die Freude reget sich" (BWV 36b), the fifth and final version of an interesting series of adaptations of a

letzte Fassung einer interessanten Serie von Bearbeitungen einer Kantate Bachs. Rivinus wird in den Sätzen 2 und 4 genannt. Alle Quellenmerkmale dieser Bearbeitung deuten auf das Jahr 1735. Mehr als auf die erneute Übernahme des Rektorats der Universität, die wohl erwähnt worden sein dürfte, kommt der Text auf das Glück des Rivinus'schen Hauses und auf seinen „Fest- und Gnadentag" zu sprechen. So scheint die Kantate den Eintritt in sein 55. Lebensjahr zu feiern, den er mit dem 54. Geburtstag am 27. Juli 1735 beging. Diese ungewöhnliche Terminierung ist zeitüblich und für seinen 69. Geburtstag sogar belegt, an dem er ein Schmuckblatt[44] überreicht bekam, auf dem der Reim zu lesen stand:
Da RIVIN In LXX Tritt,
Freun sich Treue Kinder Mit.
        Leipzig, den 27. Jul. 1750.
Rivinus beteiligte sich auch an der Kampagne gegen Johann Christoph Gottsched, der eine Gedächtnisrede zum 100. Todestag von Martin Opitz am 20. August 1739 ausgerechnet während der Vorandacht des Bußtages gehalten hatte. Das führte zu einer Anklage bei der Regierung in Dresden, die Rivinus ausdrücklich unterstützte.

Unverändert an zweiter Stelle nennen Taufzettel und Taufbuch als Patin Christiana Sibylla Bose (1711–1749), die Freundin Anna Magdalena Bachs aus dem benachbarten Haus des verstor-

Bach cantata. Rivinus is mentioned in movements 2 and 4. Source-critical evidence suggests that this adaptation was made in 1735. Rather than concentrating on Rivinus' renewed office of rector of the university, the text centers around the happiness of his family life and on his "day of celebration and grace". Thus the cantata appears primarily to celebrate his 54th birthday (on July 27, 1735), on which he entered the 55th year of his life. This unusual choice of an anniversary was common at the time and is similarly documented for his 69th birthday, on which he was presented with a beautifully ornamented broadsheet bearing the following rhyme:[44]
"Because RIVIN enters the LXX (year),
Faithful children are happy with him.
        Leipzig, July 27, 1750."
Rivinus also participated in the polemic against Johann Christoph Gottsched, who had chosen the preparatory prayer service for the Day of Repentance to give a memorial speech on the occasion of the 100th anniversary of the death of Martin Opitz on August 20, 1739. This led to charges against Gottsched at the court in Dresden, which Rivinus supported emphatically.

The second place as godparent was given both on the baptismal slip and in the baptismal register to Christiana Sibylla Bose (1711–1749), the friend of Anna Magdalena Bach who lived

97

benen Kaufmanns Georg Heinrich Bose (1682–1731). Sie übernimmt ein zweites Mal eine Patenstelle bei einem der Bachkinder, denn ihr erstes Patentöchterchen Christiana Dorothea war 1½-jährig Ende August 1732 wieder verstorben (vgl. Taufzettel 7). Auch der an dritter Stelle fungierende Pate Johann August Ernesti inzwischen zum Rektor der Thomasschule befördert, hatte sein erstes Bachsches Patenkind schon wieder verloren; es war Johann August Abraham gewesen, der 1733 nach nur zwei Tagen Lebenszeit begraben worden war (vgl. Taufzettel 9).

Der Name Johann Christian Bach steht in der Musikgeschichte am stärksten in Verbindung mit der Epoche der musikalischen Klassik. Er ist nicht nur der weltgewandte Bach – der einzige, der grundsätzlich die Grenzen seines Vaterlandes und seiner engeren Heimat hinter sich lässt –; er ist auch derjenige, der sich innerlich am meisten von seinem Vaterhaus emanzipierte. Als jüngster Sohn und elftes Kind zweiter Ehe seiner Eltern kam er in Leipzig 1735 zu jener Zeit zur Welt, da sein Vater sich erfolgreich um die Anstellung seines Sohnes Johann Gottfried Bernhard in Mühlhausen bemüht hatte.

Im Zusammenhang mit den Erbauseinandersetzungen nach dem Tode seines Vaters kommt es zu interessanten Bemühungen; in der Erbteilung heißt es dazu:
> Und weiln der jüngste Herr Sohn, Herr Johann Christian Bach 3. *Clavire* nebst

in the neighboring house of the late merchant Georg Heinrich Bose (1682–1731). She became godparent a second time, because her first goddaughter, Christiana Dorothea, had died at the age of 1 ½-years in late August 1732 (see baptismal slip no. 7). The third godparent – Johann August Ernesti, who in the meantime had been promoted to the position of rector of the St. Thomas School – had lost his first godchild from within the Bach family; Johann August Abraham was born in 1733 and only lived for two days (see baptismal slip no. 9).

The name of Johann Christian Bach is associated in the history of music primarily with the era of classicism. He was the cosmopolitan Bach who categorically left behind the borders and limitations of his native country and homeland, and he also liberated himself most from his parental ties. The youngest son and eleventh child of Bach's second marriage, he was born in Leipzig in 1735, the time when his father had just succeeded in securing employment for his son Johann Gottfried Bernhard in Mühlhausen.

Interesting developments took place when after Johann Sebastian's death his estate was divided among his heirs; in the official documents we read:
> "The youngest son, Mr. Johann Christian Bach, received 3 claviers with a set of pedals from the late departed during his lifetime, and

Pedal von dem *Defuncto* [Verstorbenen] seelig bey Lebzeiten erhalten und bei sich hat, solches auch um deßwillen nicht in die *Specification* [Aufstellung der Hinterlassenschaft] gebracht worden, weil derselbe solche von dem *Defuncto* seelig geschenkt erhalten zu haben angeführet, und dieserwegen unterschiedene Zeügen angegeben, der Frau Wittbe auch sowohl als Herrn Altnickoln und Herr Hesemann [Vormund für Gottfried Heinrich Bach] solches wißend ist, der Herr Vormund auch daher diesen seinen Mündel etwas darinne zu vergeben billig Bedencken gefunden, gleichwohl die Kinder ersterer Ehe, Herr Willhelm Friedemann Bach, Herr Carl Philipp Emanuel Bach und Jgfr. Catharina Dorothea Bachin solche Schenkung gedachten ihren jüngsten Bruder zur Zeit nicht so gleich zugestehen wollen; So haben letztere ihre Rechte dießfalls wieder denselben auszuführen sich vorbehalten, da hingegen die Frau Wittbe, der Vormund Herr Görner [Vormund für die unmündigen Kinder] wegen seiner übrigen 3. Mündel, die Frau Altnickolin und Herr Hesemann, als *Curator* Herr Gottfried Heinrich Bachs demselben die Schenckung zugestehen, und der Ansprüche dießfallß an selbigen sich begeben.[45]

Johann Christian erhielt die drei Cembali und mit ihnen den größten Teil des Erbes. Offenbar muss er als Jüngster in besonderer Weise das Herz seines Vaters besessen haben. Es sieht auch so aus, als still has them, and accordingly these were not listed in the Specificatio, since he says he received them as a present from the deceased, and he has given the names of several witnesses of this fact; the widow as well as Mr. Altnickol and Mr. Hesemann [legal guardian of Gottfried Heinrich Bach] are aware of this, and the guardian is therefore willing to make allowances regarding his charge. The children from the first marriage, however, Wilhelm Friedemann Bach, Carl Philipp Emanuel Bach and Catharina Dorothea Bach were unwilling at the time to grant their youngest brother this gift; accordingly, they formally reserved judgement on executing their rights, while the widow, the guardian Görner [legal guardian of Bach's younger children] because of his other three charges, Mrs. Altnickol and Mr. Hesemann as guardian of Gottfried Heinrich Bach conceit this gift and give up their claims."[45]

Johann Christian retained the three harpsichords and thereby the largest part of the estate. As the youngest child, he apparently must have enjoyed his father's affection in a special way. It also appears that his brothers and sister refrained from later demands because of this preferential treatment. His brother Carl Philipp Emanuel in Berlin added to the genealogy:
 "Went, after our late father's death, to his brother C. P. E. in Berlin, who

ob es in späterer Zeit keine Forderungen seiner Geschwister wegen dieser Bevorzugung mehr gegeben habe. Sein Berliner Bruder Carl Philipp Emanuel fügte der Genealogie eigenhändig hinzu:

> Gieng nach des seel[igen]. Vaters Tode zu seinem Bruder C. P. E. nach Berlin, welcher ihn erzog u. informirte. Reiste a[nn]o. 1754 nach Italien. Ist jetzt in Engelland bey der Königin in Diensten (inter nos, machte es anders als der ehrliche Veit.).[46]

In diesen wenigen Zeilen zeigt sich sowohl die Weite dieses Lebens als auch seine Grenze. In die Weite bezieht sich Carl Philipp Emanuel selbst mit ein; er hat ihn aufgenommen, gebildet und selbständig gemacht. Dass Johann Christian dann nach Italien ging, dort nicht nur seit 1760 eine gute Stellung als Domorganist in Mailand einnahm, später, nach 1762, in England am Hof Karriere als Musikmeister der englischen Königin Charlotte machte, sondern bereits 1757 zum Katholizismus konvertierte, fordert sogar die Kritik des toleranten Carl Philipp Emanuel heraus. Wie hinter vorgehaltener Hand formuliert er seinen Einspruch: „inter nos [unter uns], machte es anders als der ehrliche Veit". Das bezieht sich unmittelbar auf das Wissen aus der Genealogie. Denn unter No.1. hatte Johann Sebastian Bach selbst für den von ihm ermittelten Urahnen Veit Bach mitgeteilt:

> ein Weißbecker in Ungern, hat im 16ten *Seculo* der *lutherischen Religion* halben aus Ungern entweichen

gave him his upbringing and his education. Journeyed in 1754 to Italy. Is now in England in the service of the Queen – between us, he has managed differently from honest Veit."[46]

These few lines describe both the greater dimensions of Johann Christian's life and its limitations. For the former Carl Philipp Emanuel signed responsible – it was he who took the younger brother in, educated him and helped him to become independent. Yet though open-minded, Carl Philipp Emanuel reacted critically not only when Johann Christian went to Italy, where in 1760 he took an excellent position as cathedral organist in Milan, and then, after 1762 moved on to a distinguished career as music master at the court of Queen Charlotte in England, but particularly when in 1757 he converted to Catholicism. Carl Philipp Emanuel voiced his objections only indirectly, however: "between us, he has managed differently from honest Veit".

This observation refers directly to the family genealogy. For there under the first heading Johann Sebastian Bach had written about his ancestor Veit Bach:

> A white-bread baker in Hungary, had to flee Hungary in the sixteenth century on account of his Lutheran religion. Hence, after having converted his property into money, so far as might be, he moved to Germany; and, finding adequate

müßen. Ist dannenhero, nachdem er seine Güter, so viel es sich hat wollen thun laßen, zu Gelde gemacht, in Teütschland gezogen; und da er in Thüringen genugsame Sicherheit vor die lutherische Religion gefunden, hat er sich in Wechmar, nahe bei *Gotha* niedergelaßen.[47] Johann Christian „machte es anders als der ehrliche Veit"; es mag für Carl Philipp Emanuel eventuell wichtig gewesen sein, zumindest im Blick auf seinen verstorbenen Vater den Weg seines jüngsten Bruder kritisch zu kommentieren. Denn Veit Bach war darin „ehrlich", dass er bereit war, um seines Glaubens willen alles zurück zu lassen, was sich nicht zu Geld machen ließ; Johann Christian ist in den Augen Carl Philipp Emanuels darin unehrlich, dass er – obgleich er von seinem Vater bereits außerordentlich begünstigt worden war – um des Geldes willen seine konfessionelle Prägung aufgibt.
Doch gerade darin sah Carl Philipp Emanuel ein Charakteristikum seines jüngsten Bruders. Am 1. Januar 1782 ist Johann Christian Bach in London mit nur 46 Jahren gestorben.

Taufzettel 11

Der Taufzettel der wohl am 29. Oktober 1737 geborenen **Johanna Carolina** (1737–1781) ist – wie Taufzettel 5 – wieder durchweg von Bach selbst geschrieben. Warum das der Fall ist, wird kaum aufzuklären sein. Eine Nottaufe wie neun Jahre zuvor liegt ganz offensichtlich nicht vor. Jedenfalls befindet Bach

security for the Lutheran religion in Thuringia, settled at Wechmar, near Gotha.[47] Johann Christian "managed differently from honest Veit". Perhaps, bearing his deceased father in mind, Carl Philipp Emanuel felt the need to comment critically on the ways of his youngest brother. For Veit Bach was "honest" with regard to the fact that for the sake of his faith he was prepared to leave behind everything that could not be turned into money. In the eyes of Carl Philipp Emanuel, Johann Christian was dishonest because he was willing – even though he had been exceptionally favored by his father – to give up his religious convictions for the sake of pecuniary gain. This Carl Philipp Emanuel saw as a typical trait of his youngest brother's character. Johann Christian Bach died in London on January 1st, 1782, only 46 years of age.

Baptismal Slip 11

The baptismal slip of **Johanna Carolina** (1737–1781), probably born on October 29, 1737, was – like baptismal slip no. 5 – again written by Bach himself. Why this was the case is difficult to determine. Obviously this was not an emergency baptism as had been the case nine years earlier. Bach was

sich zu dieser Zeit in der aufregendsten Zeit des sogenannten Präfektenstreites, jener Auseinandersetzung mit seinem Rektor Johann August Ernesti um das Recht der Berufung und Einsetzung von Präfekten für den Schülerchor. Der in durchweg wohlgeformter, schwungvoller und ausgeschriebener Schrift gefasste Taufzettel nennt wie üblich zuerst die Eltern des Kindes.

in the most exacerbating phase of the so-called "prefect" controversy at that time, the conflict with Rector Johann August Ernesti over the right to call and appoint prefects for the pupils' choir. The baptismal slip, written in an elegant and well-trained hand, displays first, as was customary, the names of the infant's parents.

[11]
Die Eltern sind:
Johann Sebastian Bach,
Königl. Pohln. und Churf. Sächs. Hoff-Compositeur,
Director Chori Musici, u. Cantor zu. S. Thomae allhier. 210
und
Anna Magdalena, gebohrne Wülckin.

Die resp: Gefattern heißen:
(1) Frau Johanna, Elisabeth, gebohrne Mehlichin,
Christian Friedrich Herrn Henrici, Königl. Pohln. u. Churf. 215
Sächs. Ober-Post Comissarii Frau Liebste.
(2) Jungfer Sophia, Carolina, seel. Herrn
Georg Heinrich Bosens zweyte Jungfer
Tochter,
(3) Herr M. Christian Weise, bey der Kirche 220
zu S. Nicolai bestmeritirter Diaconus,
und S. Theol: Baccalaureus. etc.
Das Kind soll heisen:
Johanna Carolina. etc.

Leipzig. d. 30. Octobr: 1737. 225

$No \dfrac{38}{382}$ ☿ H. L. G.

[11]

        The parents are
Johann Sebastian Bach,
Royal Polish and Electoral Saxon Court Composer.
Director Chori Musici and Cantor at St. Thomas in Leipzig.
          and
Anna Magdalena, née Wülckin.

       The godparents are
(1) Johanna, Elisabeth, née Mehlichin,
dearest wife of *Christian Friedrich* Henrici, Royal Polish and Electoral
Saxon Chief Postal Commissioner.
(2) Sophia, Carolina, second daughter
of the deceased Georg
Heinrich Bose.
(3) M. Christian Weise, distinguished
deacon at St. Nicolai and bachelor
of sacred theology.
The child's name shall be
Johanna Carolina.

Leipzig. October 30, 1737.

No $\frac{38}{382}$ ☿   H. L. G.

Erstmalig erscheint der neue Titel, den Bach im Jahr zuvor mit einem Dekret vom 19. November 1736 erhalten hatte; der Hoftitel eines „Königlich Polnischen und Kurfürstlich Sächsischen Hof-Compositeurs" mochte ihn bei den laufenden Auseinandersetzungen den Rücken gestärkt haben. Die Reihe der Paten leitet er mit einer schon damals altertümlich und feierlich wirkenden Formel ein, die den Genannten Ehrerbietung zollt: „Die respect[ive]: Gefattern heißen" (213). Die Registerzeile vermerkt die 38. Taufe im Monat Oktober und die 382. Taufe im Jahr 1737, ebenso auch den Vollzug der Taufe am Mittwoch, dem 30. Oktober, durch Diaconus Gottfried Gaudlitz (vgl. Taufzettel 8). Auf der Rückseite steht nach dem Namen des Bachkindes noch der einer „Maria Gertraute". Einen Monat vor der Taufe war Bach zu jener Erbhuldigung in Wiederau gewesen, um dem neuen Erb-, Lehen- und Gerichtsherrn Johann Christian von Hennicke aus Anlass der Übernahme der Gerichtsherrschaft eine Kantate zu musizieren, „Angenehmes Wiederau, freue dich in deinen Auen" (BWV 30a). Aus diesem Anlass musste er auch dem Amtmann Beiche aus Pegau (vgl. Taufzettel 8) wieder begegnet sein, denn dieser hatte zusammen mit einem gewissen Christian Schilling – unklar bleibt, ob es sich ebenfalls um einen Amtmann der Pegauer Gegend handelt oder um den gleichnamigen Pfarrer von Stöntzsch nahe Pegau, den

For the first time we notice the new title conferred on Bach a year earlier through a governmental decree dated November 19, 1736. The title of "Royal Polish and Electoral Saxon Court Composer" probably aided him in his current conflict. The list of godparents is introduced on the baptismal slip in a manner that even then must have appeared old-fashioned and solemn but was meant to pay homage to those named: "The respective godparents are:" (line 213). The registration line notes the 38th baptism in October and the 382nd baptism of the year 1737, as well as the fact that the baptismal service took place on Wednesday, October 30, and was conducted by Deacon Gottfried Gaudlitz (see baptismal slip no. 8). On the reverse side of the slip we find, after the name of Bach´s child, the name "Maria Gertraute". A month earlier, Bach had been in Wiederau to celebrate the new lord of the manor, Johann Christian of Hennicke, on the occasion of his assuming the local juridiction, with the cantata "Angenehmes Wiederau, freue dich in deinen Auen" (BWV 30a). On that occasion he must also have met again Bailiff Beiche of Pegau (see baptismal slip no. 8), as Beiche had initiated the festive occasion, together with Christian Schilling and Christian Friedrich Henrici, known as Picander. It remains unclear whether Schilling was another official from the vicinity of Pegau, or whether this was the

Bach von der Orgelprüfung 1731/32 her kannte – und Christian Friedrich Henrici, genannt Picander, die Huldigung initiiert. Jedenfalls scheint sich in der Bestellung der ersten Patin in vermittelter Weise die Wiederauer Angelegenheit widerzuspiegeln: Johanna Elisabeth Henrici (1707–1755) war eine gebürtige Leipzigerin; erst im Juli des Vorjahres hatte sie Christian Friedrich Henrici (1700–1764), Bachs Textdichter, geheiratet, dessen Vornamen von anderer Hand hinzugefügt (215) und der als „Königl. Pohln. u. Churf. Sächs. Ober-Post Commissari[us]" tituliert wird. Ohne einen erkennbaren Grund ordnet das Taufbuch der Thomaskirche diese erste Patin an die dritte Stelle. Als zweite Patin tritt Sophia Carolina Bose (1713–1745) an den Taufstein, zweite Tochter des verstorbenen Kaufmanns Georg Heinrich Bose (1682–1731). Durch sie wird erneut die Freundschaft mit dem Hause gegenüber unter Beweis gestellt. Schließlich übernimmt an dritter Stelle wieder ein Mitglied der Familie des inzwischen verstorbenen Thomaspastors Christian Weise (1671–1736) ein Patenamt: Christian Weise d. J. (1703–1743).

Bereits mit der Bestellung der Schwester dieses Paten für Johann Christoph Friedrich (vgl. Taufzettel 8) im Jahr 1732 hatte Bach sich der nächstjüngeren Generation des ehrwürdigen Thomaspastors und familiären Beichtvaters genähert. Dass Weise d. Ä. nie selbst unter den Paten auftaucht,

parson from Stöntzsch near Pegau, whom Bach knew from his organ examination in 1731/32. In any case, the Wiederau festivities seem to be reflected in the naming of the first godparent: Johanna Elisabeth Henrici (1707–1755), a resident of Leipzig since her birth. In July of the previous year she had married Christian Friedrich Henrici (1700–1764), Bach's lyricist, whose Christian name was inserted by another hand on the baptismal slip (line 215) and who was identified as "Royal Polish and Electoral Saxon Chief Postal Commissioner (*Ober-Post Commissarius*). Without a clear reason the baptismal register of St. Thomas put this first godparent in third place. As second godparent, Sophia Carolina Bose (1713–1745), the second daughter of the deceased merchant Georg Heinrich Bose (1682–1731), went to the baptismal font, underscoring the friendship of the Bach family with the neighbor family across the square. Finally, a member of the family of the late pastor of St. Thomas, Christian Weise (1671–1736), assumed the role of godfather: Christian Weise the younger (1703–1743).

With the naming of Weise's sister as godparent for Johann Christoph Friedrich (see baptismal slip no. 8) in 1732, Bach had included the younger generation of the venerable pastor of St. Thomas and the family of the spiritual counsel of the Bach family. The fact that Weise's father never served

Christian Weise d.J. (1703–1743), Pfarrer der Nikolaikirche

Christian Weise the younger (1703–1743), pastor at St. Nikolai

gibt jene charakteristische Weise der Distanz wieder, die man damals zu Personen hielt, die einem in geistlicher Pflicht gegenüber standen. Bach gibt Weise d.J. mit allen Titeln und Funktionen an, die dieser auf sich versammelt hatte: Magister der Philosophie, Baccalaureus der Theologie und Diaconus an der Nikolaikirche.

Christian Weise d.J. war neben zwei Schwestern der einzige Sohn, der aus einer größeren Schar von

as godparent illustrates the characteristic reserve kept at that time toward individuals who were involved in one's spiritual guidance. Bach included all of Weise's titles and functions: master of philosophy, bachelor of theology, and deacon at the Nikolai Church.

Christian Weise the younger, was the only son of a large number of siblings who, together with two sisters, reached adulthood. After he had been educated by private tutors, in 1719

Geschwistern das Erwachsenenalter erreicht hatte. Nach privater Unterrichtung ließen ihn seine Eltern mit 16 Jahren 1719 an der Universität inskribieren. Bereits 1720 erwarb er das philosophische Baccalaureat und 1723 den Magistertitel. 1725 ließ er sich im Dresdner Oberkonsistorium als Kandidat der Theologie examinieren, um 1726 das theologische Baccalaureat zu erhalten. Während dieser Jahre disputierte er mehrfach, zuerst in der Philosophischen, später in der Theologischen Fakultät. Seit dem letztgenannten Jahr hielt er auch theologische Vorlesungen. Als Mitglied des Donnerstägigen Predigerkollegiums und des Collegium Philobiblicum wurde er zu Gottesdiensten in der Universitätskirche herangezogen. In der Folge bekleidete er verschiedene Kirchenstellen an St. Petri – 1729 die Nachfolge des Oberkatecheten Adam Bernd, als dieser zurücktreten musste –, an St. Thomas und St. Nikolai. 1732 verheiratete er sich mit Dorothea Elisabeth Zeh, mit der er acht Kinder hatte. Zu Pfingsten 1739 hielt er anlässlich der 200-Jahrfeier der Einführung der Reformation in Sachsen die Festansprache in der Universitätskirche. Für dieses Jubiläum brachte er außerdem eine Neuausgabe der lutherischen Bekenntnisschriften heraus. Kurz darauf erreichte er die Lizenziatenpromotion und erhielt eine außerordentliche

his parents enrolled him, at the age of 16, at the university. He received the bachelor's degree in philosophy in 1720, and the master's degree in 1723. In 1725 he passed the ministerial examination at the *Oberkonsistorium* (High Consistory) in Dresden as a candidate of theology and one year later received the bachelor's degree in theology. During that time he engaged in numerous academic disputations, first in the philosophical, later in the theological faculty. From 1725 he lectured in theology at the university. A member of the Thursday Preachers' Council and the *Collegium Philobiblicum*, he conducted services in the university church. Later he occupied positions at St. Petri, – in 1729 he succeeded the exceedingly popular preacher Adam Bernd, who had been forced to resign – at St. Thomas, and at St. Nikolai. In 1732 he married Dorothea Elisabeth Zeh, with whom he had eight children. On Whitsunday of 1739 he gave the plenary address in the university church on the occasion of the 200th anniversary of the introduction of the Reformation in Saxony. On the occasion of this anniversary he also published a new edition of the Lutheran Confessional Writings. Soon afterwards he was awarded the Licentiate degree and received a professorship in theology. In February of 1741 he was awarded the theological doctorate and was appointed

Professur an der Theologischen Fakultät. Im Februar 1741 erwarb er den theologischen Doktortitel und wurde Archidiaconus von St. Nikolai. Als solcher galt er als Hoffnungsträger der Theologischen Fakultät und hätte gewiss auch alle Erwartungen, die an ihn gestellt wurden, erfüllt. Doch starb er plötzlich und völlig entkräftet am 25. April 1743.

Johanna Carolina Bach blieb unverheiratet. Nach ihres Vaters Tod – sie ist zu diesem Zeitpunkt reichlich 12½ Jahre alt – wird sie mit den Anteilen im Testament bedacht, die ihr rechnerisch zustehen. Von dem theologischen Buchbestand ihres Vaters, der nach dem Los verteilt wurde, erhielt sie Predigtbände von Heinrich Müller, Johann Müller sowie den „Haupt-Schlüssel über die hohe Offenbarung S. Johannes" von Caspar Heunisch. Zunächst wohnte sie zusammen mit ihrer Mutter und ihrer jüngeren Schwester auf der Hainstraße, eventuell im Graffschen Hause „Zum blauen und goldenen Stern".[48] Nach dem Tod der Mutter lebte sie am Neukirchhof zusammen mit ihrer jüngeren Schwester Elisabeth Juliana Friederica Altnickol (Taufzettel 3), die aus Naumburg als Witwe zurückgekehrt war. Johanna Carolina starb eine reichliche Woche vor ihrer mehr als zehn Jahre älteren Schwester, der Altnickolin, am 16. August 1781[49] vermutlich an einer Seuche, die damals Leipzig fest im Griff hatte und viele Opfer forderte.

archdeacon at St. Nikolai. He was seen as a beacon of hope in the theological faculty and surely would have met these expectations, but he died unexpectedly from exhaustion on April 25, 1743.

Johanna Carolina Bach remained unmarried. After her father's death – she was 12 1/2 years old at that time – she received from his estate the exact share to which she was entitled. From her father's theological library, which was distributed by lot, she received sermon volumes by Heinrich Müller, Johann Müller as well as the "Hauptschlüssel über die hohe Offenbarung S. Johannes" by Caspar Heunisch. At first she lived with her mother and her younger sister on Hainstraße, perhaps in Graff's house which was named "the blue and golden Star."[48] After her mother's death she lived at the Neukirchhof with her younger sister Elisabeth Juliana Friederica Altnickol (see baptismal slip no. 3), who had returned from Naumburg as a widow. Johanna Carolina died a week before sister (who was ten years her senior), on August 16, 1781, presumably of an epidemic that had gripped Leipzig at that time and resulting in numerous deaths.[49]

Taufzettel 12

Der Taufzettel für die jüngste Tochter Bachs **Regina Susanna** (1742–1809) weist besondere Merkmale auf: Sein Format ist nur halb so groß wie die anderen; geschrieben ist er von Oberleichenschreiber Andreas Gottlieb Bienengräber; die Registriernummern sind mit roter Tinte eingetragen; Bach selbst hat keinen Anteil an dem Dokument. Sein Hoftitel wird mit „Königl. Pohln. Hof Componist" wiedergegeben.

Baptismal Slip 12

The baptismal slip for the youngest Bach daughter, **Regina Susanna** (1742–1809), has several special features. It is half the size of the other slips and was written by the senior death registrar Andreas Gottlieb Bienengräber. The registration numbers are entered with red ink. Bach himself did not contribute to the document. His title is listed as "Royal Polish Court Composer."

[12]   *Leipzig den 22. Febr 1742.*
Der Vater H. Johann Sebastian Bach, Königl Pohln.   230
Hof Componist, und Cantor zu St. Thomae.
Die Mutter, Fr. Anna Magdalena, geb. Wülckin.

Des Kindes Nahme
Regina Susanna.

Die Pathen.   235
1. *Jfr. Anna Regina, H. George Heinrich*
   Bosens, weyl Handelsm alhier, hinterl. 3te *Jfr*
   Tochter.
2. *H. D. Heinrich Friedrich Graf, Jur. Pract.*
   und Oberhofger. Advocat.   240
3. *Jfr Susanna Elisabeth H. George Heinrich*
   Bosens weyl. Handelsm. alhier hinterl
   4te *Jfr Tochter.*

No $\dfrac{30}{70}$ ⚷ H. M. E.   245

[12]   *Leipzig, February 22, 1742.*
The father is Johann Sebastian Bach, Royal Polish
Court Composer and Cantor at St. Thomas.
The mother is Anna Magdalena, née Wülckin.

The child's name is
Regina Susanna.

The godparents are.
1. *Anna Regina, third daughter of*
   the deceased merchant George Heinrich
   Bose.
2. *Dr. Heinrich Friedrich Graf, attorney*
   at the supreme court.
3. *Susanna Elisabeth, fourth daughter of*
   the deceased merchant George Heinrich
   Bose.

No $\dfrac{30}{70}$ ♃   H. M. E.

Die Wahl der Paten beschränkt sich auf das Bose'sche Haus: Die erstgenannte Patin ist Anna Regina Bose (1716–1750), die dritte der Töchter des verstorbenen Kaufmanns Georg Heinrich Bose von gegenüber. Neben ihr steht an zweiter Patenstelle D. Heinrich Friedrich Graff (1713–1777), Juris Practicus und – ebenso wie einst sein gleichnamiger Vater (vgl. Taufzettel 1) – Advokat am Oberhofgericht in Leipzig. Er hatte an der Universität Leipzig studiert und hier auch 1734 promoviert. Nun stand er nicht nur als

The choice of the godparents was restricted to the Bose family. The first godparent was Anna Regina Bose (1716–1750), the third daughter of the deceased merchant Georg Heinrich Bose of the neighboring house. Next to her, as the second godparent, was D. Heinrich Friedrich Graff (1713–1777), attorney and – just like once his homonymous father (see baptismal slip no. 1) – advocate at the supreme court of justice in Leipzig. He had studied at the University of Leipzig, where he received his

Pate neben der genannten Bose-Tochter, sondern auch als deren Verlobter, denn knapp sechs Wochen später würde er sich mit ihr verheiraten. Hier wiederholt sich eine Situation – zu dieser Zeit gern praktiziert, nämlich Verlobte gemeinsam zu Paten zu bitten –, die einst Johann Sebastian Bach und Anna Magdalena Wilcke als verlobtes Paar in Köthen zehn Wochen vor ihrer Hochzeit selbst erlebten.[50] Die dritte Patenstelle erhielt die vierte Tochter aus dem Hause Bose, Susanna Elisabeth (1718–1745), die lebenslang unverheiratet blieb. Die Registrierzeile nennt die 30. Taufe im Februar und die 70. Taufe im laufenden Jahr 1742. Taufpfarrer am Donnerstag nach Reminiscere, 22. Februar 1742, war Subdiaconus M. Christian Gottlob Eichler (1711–1785).

Christian Gottlob Eichler stammte als Pfarrerssohn aus dem Osterzgebirge und kam über die Meißner Fürstenschule St. Afra 1729 auf die Leipziger Universität. Bereits mit 22 Jahren wurde er Vesperprediger an der Universitätskirche und durchlief verschiedene Stellen an St. Petri, St. Thomas und St. Nikolai. Seit 1751 Doktor der Theologie, wurde er 1755 Pastor an der Nikolaikirche. Er gehörte neben dem Superintendenten Deyling zu den Ratswahlpredigern des letzten Lebensjahrzehnts Bachs. Anlässlich der Erbteilung erhielt Regina Susanna Bach neben Bargeld, Hausgeräten und Kleidung aus dem theologischen Buchbestand ihres

doctorate in 1734. He was not merely a godparent alongside Bose's daughter, but also her fiancé, for some six weeks later the two were married. Their choise as godparents represented a widespread custom at the time, to ask both sides of an engaged couple to be godparents. This had also happened to Johann Sebastian Bach and Anna Magdalena Wilcke when they were engaged in Köthen ten weeks before their wedding.[50] The third godparent was the fourth Bose daughter, Susanna Elisabeth (1718–1745) who was single and in fact never married. The registration line mentions the 30th baptism in February and the 70th baptism of the year 1742. The baptizing pastor on this Thursday after Reminiscere, February 22, 1742, was Assistant Deacon Christian Gottlob Eichler (1711–1785). Christian Gottlob Eichler was the son of a pastor from the eastern part of the Erzgebirge region. After attending the school of St. Afra in Meißen, he matriculated at the university in Leipzig in 1729. At the age of only 22 he became vespers preacher at the university church and subsequently held different positions at St. Petri, St. Thomas, and St. Nikolai. In 1751 he received the doctorate in theology and in 1755 he was appointed pastor at St. Nikolai. Together with Superintendent Deyling he was one of the pastors appointed to preach at town council elections during the last decade of Bach's life.

Vaters die achtbändige Jenenser Lutherausgabe in Folio. Nach ihres Vaters Tod lebte sie zunächst mit ihrer verwitweten Mutter und ihren Schwestern zusammen, teilte mit ihnen die Wohnung auf der Hainstraße, auf dem Neukirchhof und wohnte zuletzt allein auf der Quergasse. Sie blieb bis zu ihrem Tode unverheiratet. Nicht nur der Verlag Breitkopf & Härtel und der Herausgeber der Allgemeinen Musikalischen Zeitung, Johann Friedrich Rochlitz (1769–1742), setzten sich für die in ärmlichen Verhältnissen Lebende ein und sammelten Geldspenden zu ihrem Unterhalt. Auch Ludwig van Beethoven beabsichtigte, sich durch eine neue Komposition und ein Benefizkonzert zu beteiligen,[51] was aber nicht zustande kam. Auch der Schweizer Musikverleger, Komponist und Pädagoge Hans Georg Nägeli (1773–1836) versuchte, über die letzte lebende Bach-Tochter an Bachsche Autografen heranzukommen,[52] um sie in einer eigenen Bachedition zu publizieren.

Als Regina Susanna Bach gestorben war, lebten in Leipzig nur noch wenige weibliche Nachkommen[53] ihrer Schwester Elisabeth Juliana Friederica Altnickol: die Tochter Juliane Wilhelmine Prüfer, geborene Altnickol (1754–1818), die Enkelin Christiana Johanna Müller, geborene Ahlefeldt (1780–1816) und deren Tochter Augusta Wilhelmina Emma Müller (1809–1818). Doch seit

When her father's estate was distributed, Regina Susanna Bach received, in addition to cash, various houshold items and clothing, the eight-volume Jena folio edition of Luther's works from her father's theological library. After her father's death she first lived with her widowed mother and her sisters, sharing the flat on Hainstraße then at the Neukirchhof. Toward the end of her life she lived alone in Quergasse. She remained unmarried. When her distressing financial circumstances became known, this prompted the publishing house of Breitkopf & Härtel and the publisher of the *Allgemeine Musikalische Zeitung*, Johann Friedrich Rochlitz (1769–1742), to support her and solicit donations for her livelihood. Ludwig van Beethoven meant to contribute a new composition for a charity concert, which did not take place, however.[51] The Swiss music publisher, composer and educator Hans Georg Nägeli (1773–1836) sought to obtain autographs of Bach from this last surviving daughter, intending and to publish them in a special Bach edition.[52] At the time of Regina Susanna Bach's death, only a few female descendants of her sister Elisabeth Juliana Friederica Altnickol still lived in Leipzig: Her daughter Juliane Wilhelmine Prüfer, née Altnickol (1754–1818), her granddaughter Christiana Johanna Müller, née Ahlefeldt (1780–1816), and Christiana Johanna's daughter Augusta Wilhelmina Emma Müller (1809–1818).[53] Yet the early

dem Tode dieses knapp neunjährigen Mädchens gibt es in Leipzig keine Mitglieder dieser Familie mehr.

· · · · · · · ·

Die vorgestellten Taufzettel künden jedoch in jedem Falle vom Leben, da sie von der Hineinnahme von Menschen in den Leib Christi Zeugnis ablegen. Als solche wollen sie Kommentar zum Leben Bachs sein, der durch seine Kunst diesen Christus bekannte, wie in seiner Weimarer Osterkantate (BWV 31, Satz 5):
Ein Christe flieht ganz eilend von dem Grabe ... und will mit Christo lebend sein.

death of this girl at the age of barely nine years ended the association of the Bach family with the town of Leipzig.

· · · · · · · ·

The baptismal slips of St. Thomas, nonetheless, speak of life, as they give evidence of the incorporation of individuals into the body of Christ. As such they deserve to be seen as a commentary on the life of Johann Sebastian Bach, who through his great gifts bore witness to Christ, as expressed in his Weimar Easter cantata (BWV 31, set 5): A Christian flees hurriedly from the grave ... wishing to be alive with Christ.

Anmerkungen:
1. Stiehl 1979: 8, Anm. 6.
2. Bach-Dokumente, Bd. II, Nr. 630.
3. Bach-Dokumente, Bd. I, Nr. 23.
4. Bach-Dokumente, Bd. I, Nr. 25 und 26.
5. Freyse 1952: 103.
6. Freyse 1952: 116.
7. Freyse 1952: 110.
8. Freyse 1952: 110–111, unterstellte, dass dieser letzte unvollendete Geschwistername sich „auf das jüngstgeborene Schwesterlein beziehen" wird: „Elisabeth Juliane Friderica, die am 5.4.1726 geboren wurde. Dem großen Bruder [gemeint ist der unbekannte Schreiber, den Freyse mit Johann Gottfried Bernhard identifiziert] war vermutlich nur der Kosename des Rufnamens: ›Friedelena‹ geläufig; als er die übrigen Vornamen schreiben wollte, merkte er seine Unsicherheit und brach in der Mitte des nächsten ab."
9. Das am 15.11.1718 geborene und am 28.9.1719 bereits wieder verstorbene siebente Kind erster Ehe, Leopold August Bach, tritt ebenso wenig in den Blick des kindlichen Schreibers wie die Zwillinge Johann Christoph und Maria Sophie (geb. 23.2.1713), vgl. Bach-Dokumente, Bd. II, Dok. 94 und 96, sowie Dok. 56 und 57.
10. Bach-Dokumente, Bd. II, Nr. 207.
11. Bach-Dokumente, Bd. I, Nr. 42.
12. Beide Kinder erhielten die Nottaufe, Maria Sophia durch den Diakon Georg Wilhelm von der Lage, Johann Christoph durch die Hebamme, vgl. Bach-Dokumente, Bd. II, Nr. 56.

Notes:
1. Stiehl 1979: 8, note 6.
2. Bach-Dokumente, vol. II, no. 630.
3. Bach-Dokumente, vol. I, no. 23.
4. Bach-Dokumente vol. I, nos. 25 and 26.
5. Freyse 1952: 103.
6. Freyse 1952: 116.
7. Freyse 1952: 110.
8. Freyse 1952:110–11 surmised that this last, incomplete name of a sibling "referred to the youngest sister, Elisabeth Juliane Friderica", who was born on April 5, 1726. The older brother [i.e. the unknown writer whom Freyse identifies as Johann Gottfried Bernhard] presumably was familiar only with the term of endearment "Friedelena". When he proceeded to record the other given names, he realized his uncertainty and stopped in the middle of the next name.
9. The seventh child of the first marriage, Leopold August Bach, born November 15, 1718 and died September 28, 1719, received as little attention from the recording child as did the twins Johann Christoph and Maria Sophie (born February 23, 1713). See Bach-Dokumente, vol. II, nos. 94 and 96, as well as nos. 56 and 57.
10. Bach-Dokumente, vol. II, no. 207.
11. Bach-Dokumente, vol. I, no. 42.
12. Both infants received emergency baptism, Maria Sophia from Deacon Georg Wilhelm von der Lage, Johann Christoph from the midwife, cf. Bach-Dokumente, vol. II, no. 56.
13. Bach-Dokumente, vol. II, no. 207.
14. Bach-Dokumente, vol. II, no. 138.

13 Bach-Dokumente, Bd. II, Nr. 207.
14 Bach-Dokumente, Bd. II, Nr. 138.
15 Bach-Dokumente, Bd. I, Nr. 184, Genealogie No. 48.
16 Die Briefentwürfe, Brief 24.
17 E. H. Albrecht 1799: 428.
18 Verfahren gegen Adam Bernd, der sich dem Irrlehre-Vorwurf ausgesetzt sah; den Namen Melodius gebrauchte Bernd als Pseudonym.
19 Adam Bernd: Eigene Lebens-Beschreibung, Leipzig 1738, S. 204.
20 Zitiert nach: Deutsches Wörterbuch von Jacob und Wilhelm Grimm IV. Bandes erste Abtheilung, zweiter Theil. Leipzig 1897, Sp. 3003.
21 Bach-Dokumente, Bd. II, Nr. 188, Kommentar.
22 Andächtiger Seelen geistliches Brand- und Gantz-Opfer, Leipzig 1697, Vorrede von Diaconus M. Johann Günther (1660–1714), § 16. Der Buchdrucker und Verleger Andreas Zeidler (†1736), von dem hier die Rede ist, hatte seine Wohnung und Firma am Brühl, wie aus der Leichenabkündigung vom 7. Oktober 1736 in St. Nikolai hervorgeht: Nikolai-Archiv, Leichenabkündigungen, Signatur: I F 23.
23 Bach-Dokumente, Bd. II, Nr. 247.
24 Bach-Dokumente, Bd. II, Nr. 204.
25 Bach-Dokumente, Bd. II, Nr. 615; diese Äußerung Küstners macht die gesamte These von der „Kapellmeisterpartei" fraglich, vgl. Ulrich Siegele, Bachs Stellung in der Leipziger Kulturpolitik seiner Zeit (Fortsetzung), in: BJ 70,1984, S. 19 und 39.

15 Bach-Dokumente, vol. I, no. 184, Genealogie no. 48.
16 Die Briefentwürfe, letter 24.
17 E. H. Albrecht 1799: 428.
18 Legal proceedings against Adam Bernd, who was accused of heresy. Bernd used the name "Melodius" as a pseudonym.
19 Adam Bernd: Eigene Lebens-Beschreibung, Leipzig 1738, p. 204.
20 As quoted in Deutsches Wörterbuch von Jacob und Wilhelm Grimm, IV. Bandes erste Abtheilung, zweiter Theil. Leipzig 1897, col. 3003.
21 Bach-Dokumente, vol. II, no. 188, commentary.
22 Andächtiger Seelen geistliches Brand- und Gantz-Opfer, Leipzig 1697, preface of Deacon M. Johann Günther (1660–1714), § 16. The printer and publisher Andreas Zeidler († 1736) had his apartment and business in the Brühl neighborhood of Leipzig; see also the death register for October 7, 1736 in St. Nikolai: Nikolai Archiv, Leichenabkündigungen, signature: I F 23.
23 Bach-Dokumente, vol. II, no. 247.
24 Bach-Dokumente, vol. II, no. 204.
25 Bach-Dokumente, vol. II, no. 615; Küstner's remark renders the thesis of a "kapellmeister party" questionable; cf. Ulrich Siegele, Bachs Stellung in der Leipziger Kulturpolitik seiner Zeit (Fortsetzung), in: BJ 70 (1984), pp. 19 and 39.
26 Bach-Dokumente, vol. II, no. 204.
27 Hübner 2004: 110.
28 Bach-Dokumente, vol. II, no. 237.
29 Bach-Dokumente, vol. II, no. 247.

26 Bach-Dokumente, Bd. II, Nr. 204.
27 Hübner 2004: 110.
28 Bach-Dokumente, Bd. II, Nr. 237.
29 Bach-Dokumente, Bd. II, Nr. 247.
30 Agenda, das ist: Kirchen-Ordnung, wie sich die Pfarrherren und Seelsorger in ihren Aemtern und Diensten verhalten sollen ..., Leipzig 1712, S. 21–28.
31 H.-J. Schulze: Studien zur Bach-Überlieferung im 18. Jahrhundert, Leipzig/Dresden 1984, S. 97–100.
32 Bach-Dokumente, Bd. II, Nr. 273a.
33 Vgl. dazu Gerd Quedenbaum, Der Verleger und Buchhändler Johann Heinrich Zedler 1706-1751. Ein Buchunternehmer in den Zwängen seiner Zeit. Hildesheim und New York 1977, bes. S. 57–83.
34 Bach-Dokumente, Bd. II, Nr. 314.
35 Bach-Dokumente, Bd. I, Nr. 123. Vgl. dazu auch Hans Besch: Eine Auktionsquittung J. S. Bachs, in: Festschrift für Friedrich Smend zum 70. Geburtstag, Berlin 1963, S. 74–79.
36 Bach-Dokumente, Bd. I, Nr. 19.
37 Von 1746 an wird er die von Löscher begründete theologische Zeitschrift „Fortgesetzte Sammlung von Alten und Neuen Theologischen Sachen" herausgeben.
38 Vgl. A. Dürr [Hrsg.], Johann Sebastian Bach, Messe in h-Moll, BWV 232, Faksimile der autographen Partitur. Kassel und Leipzig 1965, S. 7.
39 Nikolai-Archiv Leipzig, Land-Trauer 1733 Betr., Sign.: I E 3, fol. 57v–58v.
40 Bach-Dokumente, Bd. II, Nr. 328.

30 Agenda, das ist: Kirchen-Ordnung, wie sich die Pfarrherren und Seelsorger in ihren Aemtern und Diensten verhalten sollen ..., Leipzig 1712, pp. 21–28.
31 H.-J. Schulze: Studien zur Bach-Überlieferung im 18. Jahrhundert, Leipzig/Dresden 1984, pp. 97–100.
32 Bach-Dokumente, vol. II, no. 273a.
33 Cf. Gerd Quedenbaum, Der Verleger und Buchhändler Johann Heinrich Zedler 1706–1751. Ein Buchunternehmer in den Zwängen seiner Zeit. Hildesheim and New York 1977, esp. pp. 57–83.
34 Bach-Dokumente, vol. II, no. 314.
35 Bach-Dokumente, vol. I, no. 123. Cf. also Hans Besch: Eine Auktionsquittung J. S. Bachs, in: Festschrift für Friedrich Smend zum 70. Geburtstag, Berlin 1963, pp. 74–79.
36 Bach-Dokumente, vol. I, no. 19.
37 From 1746 onwards he published the theological journal "Fortgesetzte Sammlung von Alten und Neuen Theologischen Sachen" founded by Löscher.
38 Cf. A. Dürr, ed., Johann Sebastian Bach, Messe in h-Moll, BWV 232, Faksimile der autographen Partitur. Kassel and Leipzig 1965, p. 7.
39 Nikolai Archiv Leipzig, Land-Trauer 1733, Sign.: I E 3, fol. 57v–58v.
40 Bach-Dokumente, vol. II, no. 328.
41 Nikolai-Archiv Leipzig, Leichenabkündigungen, entry for July 6, 1732; Sign: I F 23.
42 Bach-Dokumente, vol. II, no. 383, commentary.

41 Nikolai-Archiv Leipzig, Leichenabkündigungen, Abkündigung vom 6. Juli 1732; Sign.: I F 23.
42 Bach-Dokumente, Bd. II, Nr. 383, Kommentar.
43 Bach-Dokumente, Bd. II, Nr. 341.
44 Johannes Hohlfeld: Leipziger Geschlechter, Bd. 2, Leipzig 1937, S. 83. Abbildung des Blattes in: M. Petzoldt und Joachim Petri, Ehre sei dir Gott gesungen. Bilder und Texte zu Bachs Leben als Christ und sein Wirken für die Kirche. Berlin 1990², S. 15, Abb. 235.
45 Bach-Dokumente, Bd. II, Nr. 628.
46 Bach-Dokumente, Bd. I, Nr. 184, Genealogie, Hinzufügung zu No. 50.
47 Ebd. S. 255.
48 Werner Neumann: Eine Leipziger Bach-Gedenkstätte, in: BJ 56 (1970), S. 24 (19–31).
49 Hübner 2004: S. 108 und 124.
50 Bach-Dokumente, Bd. II, Nr. 108.
51 Bach-Dokumente, Bd. III, Nr. 1034.1044.
52 Detlef Gojowy: Wie entstand Hans Georg Nägelis Bach-Sammlung? Dokumente zur Bach-Renaissance im 19. Jahrhundert, in: BJ 56 (1970), S. 66–104.
53 Hübner 2004: S. 132–136.

43 Bach-Dokumente, vol. II, no. 341.
44 Johannes Hohlfeld: Leipziger Geschlechter, vol. 2, Leipzig 1937, p. 83. Illustration in: M. Petzoldt and Joachim Petri, Ehre sei dir Gott gesungen. Bilder und Texte zu Bachs Leben als Christ und sein Wirken für die Kirche. Berlin 1990, p. 15, illus. 235.
45 Bach-Dokumente, vol. II, no. 628.
46 Bach-Dokumente, vol. I, no. 184, Genealogie, addition to no. 50.
47 Ibid., p. 255.
48 Werner Neumann: Eine Leipziger Bach-Gedenkstätte, in: BJ 56 (1970), p. 24 (19–31).
49 Hübner 2004: pp. 108 and 124.
50 Bach-Dokumente, vol. II, no. 108.
51 Bach-Dokumente, vol. III, no. 1034.1044.
52 Detlef Gojowy: Wie entstand Hans Georg Nägelis Bach-Sammlung? Dokumente zur Bach-Renaissance im 19. Jahrhundert, in: BJ 56 (1970), pp. 66–104.
53 Hübner 2004: pp. 132–136.

Literatur

Erdmann Hannibal Albrecht: Sächsische evangelisch-luthersche Kirchen- und Predigergeschichte von ihrem Ursprunge an bis auf gegenwärtige Zeiten. Erster Band. Diöces Leipzig, Leipzig 1799. Nach E. H. Albrechts Tode fortgesetzt von M. Johann Friedrich Köhler. Ersten Bandes zweite Fortsetzung. Diöces Leipzig, Leipzig 1802.
Maria Hübner (Hrsg.): Anna Magdalena Bach. Ein Leben in Dokumenten und Bildern. Mit einem biographischen Essay von H.-J. Schulze, Leipzig 2004.
Bach-Dokumente, Bd. I: Schriftstücke von der Hand Johann Sebastian Bachs, vorgelegt und erläutert von W. Neumann und H.-J. Schulze, Leipzig 1963.
Bach-Dokumente, Bd. II: Fremdschriftliche und gedruckte Dokumente zur Lebensgeschichte J. S. Bachs 1685–1750, von W. Neumann und H.-J. Schulze, Kassel und Leipzig 1969.
Bach-Dokumente, Bd. III: Dokumente zum Nachwirken Johann Sebastian Bachs 1750–1800, vorgelegt und erläutert von H.-J. Schulze. Kassel und Leipzig 1972.

Die Briefentwürfe des Johann Elias Bach (1705–1755), herausgegeben und kommentiert von E. Odrich und P. Wollny, Hildesheim/Zürich/New York 2005.
Conrad Freyse: Die Schulhefte Wilhelm Friedemann Bachs, in: BJ 39 (1951–1952), S. 103–119.
Karl Geiringer: Die Musikerfamilie Bach. Leben und Wirken in drei Jahrhunderten, München 1958.
Johann Christoph Rost: Nachricht, Wie es, in der Kirchen Zu St: Thom: alhier, mit dem Gottes Dienst, Jährlichen so wohl an Hohen Festen, als andern Tagen, pfleget gehalten Zu werden. Leipzig 1716. Hs. Archiv der Thomaskirche.
Herbert Stiehl: Taufzettel für Bachs Kinder – ein Dokumentenfund, in: BJ 65 (1979), S. 7–18.
Christoph Wolff u.a.: Die Bach-Familie, Stuttgart und Weimar 1994.

Bildnachweis:

Bach-Archiv Leipzig: S. 20, S. 50, S. 70, S. 96
Gert Mothes (Foto): S. 1, S. 4, S. 30, S. 119
Joachim Petri (Foto): S. 77, S. 88
Stadtgeschichtliches Museum: S. 32, S. 57, S. 106
Staatsbibliothek zu Berlin: S. 82

Archiv Thomaskirche Leipzig: S. 12/13, S. 56, S. 120
Universitätsbibliothek Leipzig: S. 45 (Signatur: M 04464744)
Archiv Martin Petzoldt: S. 37, S. 91

Blick in den Chorraum mit den Superintendenten-Bildern, dem Bachgrab, dem Taufstein und dem Paulineraltar

View of the choir showing portraits of the superintendents, the Bach tomb, the babtismal font and the Altar of St. Paul

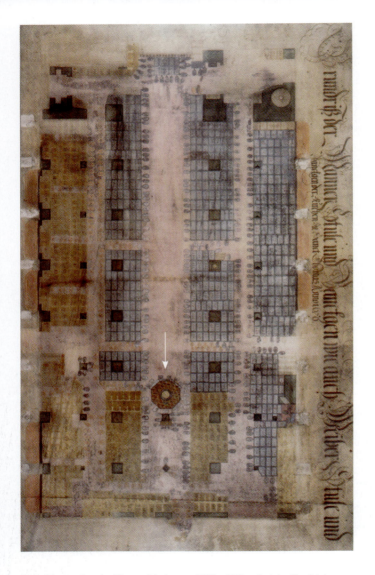

Bestuhlungsplan der Thomaskirche von 1679 mit Standort des Taufsteins unterhalb der Westempore

Seating plan of the St. Thomas Church (1679) indicating the location of the baptismal font under the western loft